CONTROLLING CASH FLOW

CONTROLLING CASH FLOW

DAVID H BANGS

KOGAN
PAGE

Kogan Page Limited acknowledge with thanks the assistance of Michael K Lawson of Windsor Management Consultants in the preparation of this edition.

First published in the United States of America in 1987
by Upstart Publishing Company Inc, Portsmouth, New Hampshire 03801, USA.

This edition first published in Great Britain in 1989 by
Kogan Page Limited, 120 Pentonville Road, London N1 9JN.

British Library Cataloguing in Publication Data
Bangs, David H. Controlling cash flow.
   1. Great Britain. Business firms. Financial
   management. Cash flows
   I. Title
   658.1′5244

   ISBN 1-85091-857-0
   ISBN 1-85091-859-7 pbk.

Typeset by DP Photosetting, Aylesbury, Bucks
Printed and bound in Great Britain by
Biddles Ltd, Guildford

◀ CONTENTS ▶

◀ TO THE READER ▶

Your business's staying power depends on maintaining a positive cash flow. Money has to come into the business at least as fast as it goes out.

This challenge confronts all small business owners.

Sometimes the problem is simple liquidity. When there isn't enough money to meet current bills (including payroll and taxes), debtors may be the problem. Every debtor is a cost to you – in effect, you are financing your customers.

Sometimes the problem is chronic, caused by lagging sales or by insufficient capital, and results in excessive borrowing needs.

Sometimes the problem is caused by slipping margins: the cost of sales goes up, contribution to overhead and profit goes down.

Sometimes the problem is seasonal. Stock purchased for resale may have to be paid for before the selling season. The terms your suppliers demand may be expensive for you to meet, so you don't take advantage of discounts.

Sometimes explosive growth is the problem. Sales become cash more slowly than you plan – so while sales are skyrocketing, so are your cash disbursements. Keeping the two in balance calls for more capital, or more debt, or both.

How do you work out what to do? Cash flow problems are complex and affect all of us. Most can be solved by taking careful, thoughtful precautions. And if cash flow problems can't be avoided altogether, they can be foreseen, and their impact on your business's survival and profitability minimised.

That's what *Controlling Cash Flow* is about. We used a real-life example, drawn from a going business that has had its normal share of cash flow problems. Finestkind Seafoods Ltd is representative of other small businesses. They have to profitably turn stock to keep going. They have to watch costs, establish budgets, face unexpected hurdles – and still meet their fixed costs and payroll in a timely way.

To make the best use of this book, modify the worksheets in the text to suit your own business, since the examples drawn from Finestkind (see Appendix 1) probably won't reflect the realities of your business. You have to tailor your forecasts, budgets and financial statements to your own needs – perhaps with the help of your accountant, or bank manager.

Follow the steps in the text and you will learn a cash flow control process. The benefits of learning this process are great. Profits will increase because your costs are lower. You will have less need for debt – but have credit available for liquidity needs if and when they arise. You can take discounts and avoid late payment charges. You can avoid cash flow crises – and be able to take advantage of opportunities as they present themselves.

The process is well proved in practice. Thousands of small businesses use it. It takes application and patience – and your knowledge of how your business works.

David H Bangs

◀ FOREWORD ▶

Upon completing my first reading of *Controlling Cash Flow*, I was struck with one thought: 'How many times during the past ten years could I have used the information presented in this book. I learned these techniques the hard way – by making mistakes which, in some cases, could have cost me the company.'

In any company, large or small, cash is the fuel needed to generate business. In fact, every major step taken by the small business owner, whether it is borrowing to support growing debtors or signing a lease on new manufacturing equipment, ends up with a decision to 'bet the business'. Unless there is adequate information available to support these decisions, your odds of making the right decision may be better at the racetrack.

In my experience, many business owners manage their affairs by the 'seat-of-the-pants' approach. If there is money in the bank, something must be going right; if there isn't, it is time to cut back. This approach tends to work well in a stable environment, when sales are relatively steady and costs seem rational, even if they are not always in control. However, when the business environment undergoes changes, the 'seat-of-the-pants' approach can make you sit down quickly.

For instance, a rapid sales growth in most businesses, no matter how well accomplished, causes a debilitating cash outflow every bit as difficult to deal with as that caused by operating losses. The typical result of this scenario is a fast unprepared trip to the bank for a short-term loan to tide the business over until sales turn to cash. The problem is that even a bank manager may not understand the cash flow problems caused by rapid sales growth, and will assume that new sales are going to vanish in a pool of bad debts or that they don't exist to begin with. To avoid these kinds of problem, make sure you have a well-thought-out, long-term financing plan. Your bank and your accountant can help you to put it together.

The only way to win at the cash flow game is to understand how your business is doing, accurately predict your future capital requirements, and then follow the plan you develop to meet those requirements. The information in *Controlling Cash Flow* will help by showing you the techniques used by financial managers in companies ranging in size from those who keep their bookkeeping records in a shoe box to public companies. Some of the techniques are not easy; you may have to get professional help in order to implement them. However, there is no substitute for them.

The first financial goal most of us set for our business is to create sustained growth and profitability. This cannot be done without understanding both the opportunities and the limitations we face every day as business owners and managers. This book will not help you to uncover opportunities, but if you find them, it will help you to plan around your limitations.

Neil C Herring

◀ INTRODUCTION ▶

Managing for cash flow is managing for survival. Manage cash flow effectively, and your business works. Costs are in order. Sales and collection efforts work together. Margins are protected, market share grows, and profits increase.

Manage cash flow effectively, and your business works.

Mismanage your cash flow, and you won't be able to do much more than struggle to stay afloat and sing the cash flow blues.

What causes cash flow blues? There are four major causes:
1. Fixed costs creep upwards;
2. Variable costs slip out of control;
3. Sales don't turn into cash fast enough;
4. Stock levels become bloated.

There are other causes – but these are the main profit killers.

This book outlines the steps you can take to improve a less than optimal cash flow. The steps involved are neither magical, mysterious nor even new. They take time and effort – but they work. In the Appendix, you will see how budgets, taken from an actual business, work.

Keep the prime aim – survival – in focus at all times. If gearing up for anticipated sales could lead to financial disaster, take your time. You can't afford to acquire excessive plant and stock or to hire people too soon. Wait. Wait until your plant is bursting at the seams, your employees are beginning to pile up overtime, and the sales are there.

Then you can expand. Not before.

Cash flow has to be managed

Start to manage your cash flow by looking at your past performance. Unless you have good reasons to expect differently, expect your business to repeat the same general patterns year after year. Your business has a momentum that's hard to change, and while you can make substantial changes for the worse very easily, making changes that improve profitability is very difficult.

Forecasts and budgets

Forecasts and budgets are so closely related that they can't be separated. Your forecasts become your budgets. To make budgeting and forecasting simpler, break them into a series of small steps.

1. What are your sales goals?

You need these for the budget period and beyond. Sales drive your business. In the long run, operating profits (sales less expenses) are far and away the most important source of cash for your business.

2. What will your expenses be?

You have to meet your fixed costs every month. Other expenses and costs are tied directly to sales, and can be calculated as a function of sales level.

3. What's going on around you?

General business and economic conditions in your market area or in your target markets, competition, new technologies, and shifts in market taste are among the many variables you have to accommodate. You want your projections to help you to set accurate goals, but those goals have to be achieved in the real world. The real world is fickle, imprecise, and has a way of tripping up the over-optimistic forecaster.

4. How do you establish budgets?

Companies without budgets invite disaster, and usually get it. Anyone can set up a budget. The trick is to set up budgets that are worth following. A cash flow budget based on your business, your products, your markets, and your experience is going to be worth following. This book can help you to set up a cash flow budget that works.

The difference between cash and working capital

Cash is the most liquid of all your current assets. It's what you use to pay all your bills.

Working capital, on the other hand, is those current assets left over after all current liabilities are met. Look at your company's balance sheet. Your current assets are listed in order of decreasing liquidity: Cash, Debtors, Prepayments, Stock, and so on. Simply stated, a cash flow problem arises when you have current liabilities to meet but no cash on hand: you can't pay bills with your debtors.

There are three ways to deal with a working capital problem:

1. Get new, permanent investment (equity) in the business

This solution may be the most desirable since it does not involve any interest expense. In addition, it solves the number-one small business problem: undercapitalisation – but it does mean that you have to put in more funds yourself or sell a part of the business to get someone else to put funds in.

2. Borrow against your debtors

You can take on short-term debt (for one year or less) without incurring excessive interest payments. This debt is repaid by the business's stock turnover.

3. Get a long-term working capital loan

This kind of loan is usually repaid out of profits over three or more years. However, there are two considerations you must keep in mind: the rate of interest may be higher; this type of loan becomes another fixed expense, thereby increasing your liabilities.

Your goal of improved profitability will only be reached by improved cash flow. Ultimately, you must weigh the advantages and disadvantages of each of these three approaches and decide which one (or ones) will work best for you.

5. How do you use the cash flow budget?

Once you have established forecasts, goals and budgets, keep on top of what the business is really doing as compared with what was forecast and budgeted. You put your budget to work through variance analysis, a simple tool that helps you spot dangers and opportunities early. If you see a trend developing before your competition does, or plug a cash flow leak by noting an expense nudging upward, you will come out ahead.

Work with your bank manager

If you are not comfortable preparing financial statements, or if you just want to improve your banking relationships, involve your bank manager in your long-range planning efforts. Bank managers are like anyone else: they like to use their skills. Since most bankers have sophisticated financial management skills, it is to your advantage to make the first move. Invite your bank manager to help you.

Be honest with him or her. If you keep communications flowing, you will increase the probability of getting the financing you really need, when you need it, and at the lowest cost.

CHAPTER 1

DETERMINE YOUR FINANCING NEEDS

At some point, no matter how carefully you monitor your cash flow, you will have to borrow: to cover a temporary cash flow gap, to grab an opportunity, or to provide working capital for growth without diluting your equity.

One of the classic ways small business owners trip themselves up is to use this year's financing to pay off last year's debts and operating losses.

Plan ahead. A written financing plan – whether for a bank's or your own use – is a major step in the right direction. Accurate cash flow projections are integral parts of your financing plan. They help you to avoid cash flow problems, anticipate financing needs (for growth or survival), and help you to keep your borrowing costs as low as possible.

Your cash flow projection will help you to provide clear, factual answers to questions such as:

1. What are my financing needs?
2. Why can't they be met from retained earnings?
3. Are operating profits going to be sufficient to meet long-term debt repayment?
4. How much do I need? When do I need it? On what terms?
5. Should I use a new loan, or is new equity investment needed?
6. How will this loan – if made – be repaid? (Or, from an investor's perspective, how will this investment be profitable?)

If the answer to your financing needs is new or increased bank borrowing, you must be able to show that you can service the loan from operating profits. One of the classic ways small business owners trip themselves up is to use this year's financing to pay off last year's debts and operating losses. This kind of pyramiding is devastating. It creates a monstrous debt load that can overwhelm profitability and keep you permanently pedalling furiously to stay in the same place. That is dispiriting, discouraging, disheartening and disastrous.

How do you put together a financing plan?

Make sure that you know your needs before going to the bank.

Start by identifying the different needs for funds. Some of these needs can be covered by operations. Those that cannot (or cannot without tripping you into illiquidity) should be carefully scrutinised to see whether they are necessary. If they are, you can turn to the question of whether or not more borrowing should be sought – or if the need might be met in some other way.

It is important to remember that if debt financing is needed to cover a cash flow gap caused by insufficient operating profits, the underlying cause must be identified and dealt with before financing will do any good. Borrowing to paper over an operating problem always leads to a worse situation, tempting though it may be at the time.

Suppose, for example, that your sales have fallen off and costs have risen, making it clear that soon you will have a severe liquidity or working capital problem. If the lag in sales can be cured without borrowing, fine. You can almost always take costs down a notch or two. If you will still have a cash flow problem, then make sure that borrowing won't make it worse. If the sales problem cannot be resolved, sooner or later you'll be back to the bank to borrow more, thus driving costs even higher. Your fixed costs are made bigger, increasing the operating loss, so the need for more debt money becomes more pressing.

And so it goes.

Make sure that you know your needs before going to the bank. Your bank manager will want to know what benefits the new borrowing will bring. Any bank manager you would want to work with will ask, almost before you sit down, what you need the money for and whether you could raise it from operations. To stammer and admit you hadn't looked for operating economies and profits as a way to generate cash is a sure way to lose credibility.

Avoid this. Enter the bank well prepared.

Five questions your financing plan should answer

Your cash flow projection will provide most of the information necessary.

1. *What do you need the loan for?* Is it working capital? New equipment? Expansion?
2. *How much is needed?*
3. *How will the money be repaid?* Document with cash flow and income projections, balance sheets, and substantial marketing and sales plans.
4. *When is the money needed?* Timing is important. You can often reduce borrowing needs by rescheduling. Some loans (such as those for property, major equipment, or any large sum that has to go to a loan committee) take time to process.
5. *What kind of financing is most appropriate for your business?* Why?

The basic rule in financing is: *Match the term of the loan to both the term of the need and the source of repayment.*

The use of an overdraft to finance long-term needs cripples a lot of businesses. Using an overdraft in lieu of permanent financing is very risky. Not only is there the ever-present danger that the facility will not be renewed, but there is the added disadvantage of never being able to plan beyond the short term.

1. Short-term needs call for short-term loans or fluctuating overdraft facilities.
2. Medium-term needs usually call for term loans.
3. Long-term needs call for both long-term debt and increased equity investment.

Figure 1.1. *Basic rule of finance*

Five types of financing

Legitimate financing needs fall into five related categories. At any one time you may need recourse to several of these. A going business with a new division is like a start-up – it may have working capital needs and will have additional equipment demands.

1. Start-ups

A new business needs a combination of invested capital and long-term debt. Capitalisation needs are detailed in the income and cash flow projections. Trade or industry figures give an idea of average capitalisation needs. Initial equipment and other fixed asset costs can be spelled out in great detail. The balance of debt to equity ('gearing') is important – too much debt too early makes future financing hard to come by.

Don't buy fixed assets on short terms.

2. Working capital shortages

After initial capitalisation, working capital is generated from operating profits over a long period. If you suffer from chronic working capital shortages due to undercapitalisation but are making some operating profits, then the answer may be a term loan. However, you must demonstrate that the loan will more than repay itself in additional operating profits. Quite often, a modest working capital loan will put a business over the hump and provide enough breathing room to make much higher operating profits. You can model the impact of the loan in your cash flow projections.

But remember, a working capital loan, which is paid back monthly over a period of three to seven years, adds substantially to your overhead costs. If your business won't generate sufficient added operating profits to cover the loan payments plus 50 to 100 per cent, then added equity is needed, not another loan.

3. Equipment and other fixed assets

Equipment and other fixed asset loans are clear examples of matching a loan to the need and repayment base. Since these loans are ordinarily secured by the equipment, the anticipated useful life of the equipment becomes a major factor in the credit decision.

A very rough guideline is that you can finance equipment with a projected useful life of 10 years for up to 70 per cent of its life, and for as much as 90 per cent of its value. Manufacturers tend to have fairly generous credit policies, but even so, you should follow these guidelines for your own safety.

Don't buy fixed assets on short-term finance. The timing is wrong. If you are trying to finance your business with sweat equity, fine. This is not the best place to put sweat equity to work. Finance it for five instead of seven years, or three instead of four.

While equipment loans rarely go beyond seven years, commercial property is often financed over 15 or more years, depending on the situation. Since you build equity in equipment and property over a number of years from profits, you want to finance it the same way.

For long-term credit, a business must demonstrate the ability to generate profits consistently.

4. Stocks and work in progress

These loans are short term and are usually tied to a clearly defined source of repayment, such as one stock turn, the fulfilment of a contract, or the sale of a specific asset. However, in practice many banks are reluctant to offer finance secured exclusively on stocks and work in progress, and most would seek personal guarantees from the proprietor of a small business as a minimum additional security.

Short-term loans are repaid from short-term sources that are clearly identified before the credit is granted.

Medium- and long-term loans, on the other hand, may be repaid from less directly identifiable sources. A banker looks to proven management ability (usually evidenced by a profitable history and clearly understood plans) for repayment. Since there is no one fast source of repayment, the risk is greater, and the decision more difficult.

This is a crucial distinction. A company may be an excellent short-term credit risk, but for long-term credit, a business must demonstrate the ability to generate profits consistently.

Remember, instalments on term loans fall due for payment every month or quarter, adding to fixed costs. As the overhead rises, so does the risk and the need for more careful management. Your bank manager recognises this. So should you.

5. Sustained growth

The final major category of bankable loans is for growth, which can outstrip working capital. A business anticipating fast growth should also anticipate a lot of danger.

As sales go up, liquidity goes down. Sales don't turn to cash as fast as suppliers need to be paid. As you add staff, productivity plummets. New, larger space is needed, with more administrative burden and increased fixed costs. It's inevitable.

The usual solution is a combination of new invested capital, lines of credit tied to debtors and stocks, and long-term working capital loans.

Notice what this implies. If you plan to grow, you must plan to generate profits consistently, at the same time keeping your business liquid to meet current obligations. At all costs, overtrading should be avoided.

To make sure that you maintain liquidity, you have to make sure of your financing. The answer? A financing plan based on thorough income and cash flow projections.

CHAPTER 2

PREPARE SALES AND EXPENSE FORECASTS

Cash flow control starts with sales and expense forecasts. These provide the basic data for both income and cash flow projections, which are the primary budgeting tools.

If you can count on one thing, it's that business situations change constantly.

The simplest approach is to extrapolate current sales, using historical financial data as a guideline. The problem with such an approach is that it doesn't take change into account – and if you can count on one thing, it's that business situations change constantly.

A better technique involves breaking your goods and services into several product lines, then using Figure 2.1: *Sales forecasting* to arrive at a 'most likely' figure.

Begin by assuming the worst. In the column headed 'low', put down the sales you would expect if everything went wrong – poor weather, loss of market share to a new competitor, your star salesperson going to your most hated competitor (taking along his or her accounts), new product competition you can't match, and so on.

Then – this is more fun – assume that everything works out the way you wish. Put down your rosiest hopes in the column headed 'high'. All your promotional efforts will succeed, markets will grow explosively, your competitors will stub their toes and slink away from the market, your suppliers will fill your stock requirements instantaneously.

Realistically, sales will end up in between the high and low estimates. The figures here will (usually) be more accurate than a one-off estimate will be. More thought has gone into their preparation.

Sales forecast for the period: _____ to _____

Sales	Low	Most likely	High
Product 1:			
Product 2:			
Product 3:			
Product 4:			
Total Sales:	_____	_____	_____

Figure 2.1   *Sales forecasting*

Expense forecasts

You can use the same three-column process to forecast expenses. Most expenses are reasonably stable within a sales range.

However, a better approach takes some more subtle distinctions into account.

Expenses fall into two categories: fixed and variable.

Fixed expenses are independent of sales levels (within limits: see Figure 2.2). If sales increase dramatically, some of these expenses will explode. This 'step function' is unusual, though. If you anticipate large sales increases, you need professional advice from your bank manager and accountant to forecast expenses.

Expenses, both in absolute amounts and in management time, tend to rise in steps, not smoothly, as a percentage of sales. A modest increase in sales may greatly increase profits, because it will not affect fixed

Increased sales and increased expenses go together, but not in a smooth line, particularly in growing businesses. If you expect a substantial increase in sales over the next budgeting period, try to calculate what this will mean in terms of:

- **Operating margins.** Will they remain stable? Go lower? Higher? Why?
- **Fixed costs.** New plant and equipment may be needed. What will happen to overhead and administrative expenses? Will new debt be needed?
- **Profitability.** What will the increase do – will there be a lag? What about credit and collection expenses? Bad debt experience?

Figure 2.2 *Sales and expenses*

expenses. But a major sales increase can actually result in lowered profits – and severely (if temporary) negative cash flow – if fixed expenses take an upwards leap.

Variable costs rise and fall with sales levels, and can usually be forecast as a pecentage of sales. Your own records, plus trade figures, will give you a realistic percentage range for each variable expense.

Fixed expenses:		**Variable expenses:**	
Salaries	_____	Sales Commissions	_____
NI	_____	Packaging	_____
Rent	_____	Travel	_____
Utilities	_____	Entertainment	_____
Licences and fees	_____	Carriage	_____
Insurance	_____	Overtime	_____
Advertising	_____	Bad debt	_____
Legal and accounting	_____		
Depreciation	_____	**Mixed expenses:**	
Interest	_____	Telephone	_____
Maintenance and cleaning		Postage etc.	_____
etc.	_____		

This is not an exhaustive list. If you are undecided about which of your expenses are fixed and which are variable, check with your accountant.

Figure 2.3 *Fixed and variable expenses*

A very few expenses are mixed. Take a conservative approach and treat these as fixed expenses, unless you have good reasons to link them more closely to sales.

Now list your expenses and 'most likely' sales forecasts from Figures 2.1 and 2.3 on Figure 2.4: *Sales and expense summary*. These are gross figures, which will be broken down more finely in the following chapters.

One-year and three-year Sales and Expenses (total for each product line)

	Next year:	**Three years:**

Sales: (List your sales figures from Figure 2.1)

1.

2.

3.

4.

Expenses: (List your expenses from Figure 2.3)

1.

2.

3.

4.

Figure 2.4 *Sales and expense summary*

◀ CHAPTER 3 ▶

PREPARE PROFIT PROJECTIONS

You build your profit projections on the forecasts you just finished.

Profit projections show your anticipated revenues, expenses, and profits. They also include non-cash expenses, such as amortisation and depreciation, and show only interest paid on debts. Cash flow projections, on the other hand, show cash actually received and disbursed, and include principal plus interest paid on debts, but exclude non-cash expenses.

For most businesses (and for most bank managers), profit projections covering three years are more than adequate. In some cases, such as when you apply for a long-term loan, a longer projection may be requested. In general, though, the longer the projection, the less accurate it will be, and the less useful as a guide to action.

You don't need a crystal ball to make your projections. While no set of projections will be 100 per cent accurate, experience and practice tend to make projections more precise. Even rough projections provide a set of benchmarks to measure your progress towards short-term goals. Like a sketch map, rough projections are better than no directions at all.

If your projections are wildly incorrect, correct them. When to do this is a matter of judgement. A rule of thumb is that if a projected revenue or expense item is more than 20 per cent off for a quarter (three months), revise it. If it is less than 20 per cent off, wait for another quarter. Do not

Like a sketch map, rough projections are better than no directions at all.

Microcomputers and financial projections are meant to go together. A microcomputer and a spreadsheet program such as Supercalc or Lotus 1-2-3 take the drudgery out of setting up and then tinkering with the income, cash flow and other projected financial statements.

Your accountant or other financial advisers may have already set up a template that fills your business-forecasting needs. A template is a pre-established set of commands for a specific software program, one which has already tested the arithmetic to make sure that the finished product (the projection) accurately reflects your data and assumptions. If not, they may be able to help you use your own software.

A modelling program such as Mastermodeller™ provides an integrated approach to preparing financial projections and budgets. You enter the data in common-sense formats, and at the end of the data entry, you can print out a comprehensive set of financial projections and budgets.

All your computer program can do, however, is process information that you provide. If your assumptions are off, your projections will be, too.

What's the great advantage of these programs?

Without going through hundreds of calculations, each one of which admits the possibility of innocent arithmetic error:

1. You can revise projections instantly, remedying omissions or correcting erroneous assumptions.
2. You can test hypotheses about price, debt load, fixed costs, unit sales and so on.
3. You can create a series of projections based on different sets of assumptions.
4. You can use more sophisticated financial analyses than were possible for a small business before the computer. Ask your accountant or bank manager about using (among other tools) internal rates of return and discounted future cash flows, establishing economic ordering quantities, or using break-even analysis in making pricing decisions.
5. Budget variation analysis is greatly simplified. You can set up a program to flag automatically any projected item which exceeds the variance limits you establish, whether in percentages, cash value, or both.

In short, you have access to the level of financial management (including cash flow control) that used to be the province of big business.

Figure 3.1 *Computers and projections*

change your projections more often than quarterly. In a short period, many trends are distorted or magnified. These distortions will usually even out over a longer period. Of course, if you find you have omitted a major expense item or discover a significant new source of revenue, make immediate corrections.

The reasoning behind income projection is that since most revenues and expenses maintain the same patterns from one year to the next, the future will be much like the past. For example, if your gross margin has historically been 30 per cent of net sales, you can safely assume (barring strong evidence to the contrary) that it will continue to be 30 per cent of net sales for the immediate future.

The expense that bleeds your business dry is almost always one which was overlooked or seriously misjudged – and therefore not allowed for.

If you are starting a business, look for financial statements and financial ratios for businesses similar to yours. Business libraries and trade association figures are two good sources of 'common-sized' financial statements. (A 'common-sized' statement expresses sales, expense and balance sheet items as a percentage of total sales to facilitate comparison of a number of businesses of different sizes.) Check with your accountant and bank manager for other sources of information.

You have to be thorough and systematic when you prepare your profit projection. The expense that bleeds your business dry (makes it illiquid) is almost always one which was overlooked or seriously misjudged – and therefore unplanned for. There are some expenses which cannot be foreseen. The best way to protect your business against these is to document all your assumptions and be conservative in your estimates. 'Conservative' means to understate your anticipated revenues and overstate expenses.

It is far better to exceed a conservative estimate than to fall below optimistic projections. However, being too far under creates a special set of problems, such as not having sufficient capital to finance growth. Basing profit projections on hopes or unjustified fears is hazardous to your business's health. Be realistic.

Profit forecasts and projections can be standardised to make comparison and analysis easier. They should be dated to indicate the period of time they cover, and they should also contain notes to explain any unusual items, such as windfall profits, legal expenses and judgements, changes in depreciation rates, and other material information. Assumptions should always be footnoted – to help remind you of how the numbers were originally obtained or justified, to provide a boost up the learning curve when you review your projections, and to help improve future projections.

Every month, compare your actual income and expenses against your projected income statements. (See Chapter 5: Use the Cash Flow Budget and Variance Analysis, for details.) You want to detect deviations as soon as possible so you can correct problems before they get out of hand, and seize opportunities while they are still fresh.

Suggested formats for profit statements (and projections) are shown in Figure 3.2. You may want to modify the example by adding or deleting a few expense or revenue items to fit your particular operation, but do not change the basic format.

Remember, the purpose of financial statements and projections is to provide you with the maximum amount of useful information and guidance, not to dazzle a prospective lender or investor.

---

(1) **Net Sales:**
(2) less **Cost of Goods Sold:**
(3) equals **Gross Margin:**
(4) **Operating Expenses:**
  Salaries and wages
  PAYE and NI
  Rent
  Utilities
  Maintenance
  Office supplies
  Postage
  Car and truck
  Insurance
  Legal and professional
  Depreciation
  Others:
  _____
  _____
  _____

---

(5) **Other Expenses:**
     Interest
(6) **Total Expenses:**
(7) **Profit (Loss) Pre-Tax:**
(8) **Tax:**
(9) **Net Profit (Loss):**

Explanation of sample

(1) **Net Sales.** Gross sales less returns, allowances and discounts.
(2) **Cost of Goods Sold.** Includes cost of stock sold, but not stocks that remain unsold at the end of the period.
(3) **Gross Margin.** (1) Net Sales minus (2) Cost of Goods Sold. Represents the gross profit on sales without taking indirect costs into account.
(4) **Operating Expenses**. These are the costs which, together with (5) Other Expenses, must be met no matter what the sales level may be. The order in which they are stated is not important. Thoroughness is. If some costs are trivial, lump them together under a heading of 'miscellaneous', but be prepared to break them out if the miscellaneous totals more than an arbitrary 1 per cent of Net sales.
(5) **Other Expenses.** These are non-operating expenses. The most common is interest expense. It is helpful to display your interest expense in some detail both to highlight the cost of money and to provide easy access to information used for ratio analysis.
(6) **Total Expenses.** Sum of (4) Operating Expenses and (5) Other Expenses.
(7) **Profit (Loss) Pre-Tax.** (3) Gross Margin minus (6) Total Expenses.
(8) **Tax.** Consult your accountant or, as a rule of thumb, apply the standard rate of tax. By the time you receive the benefit of capital allowances etc you should find the real tax figure is a little lower than your estimate.
(9) **Net Profit (Loss).** (7) minus (8). This represents the success or lack thereof for your business. There are three ways to make this figure more positive: increase gross margin, decrease total expenses, or both.

For the most useful projection, state your assumptions clearly. Do not put down numbers that you cannot rationally substantiate. Do not puff your gross sales projection to make the net profit positive. Give yourself conservative sales figures and pessimistic expense figures to make the success of your deal more probable. Be realistic.

Figure 3.2 *Income statement format*

To prepare your profit projections, use the data from Chapter 2. This proceeds logically. Enter the data on a 13-column spreadsheet which is set up according to the formats of Figures 3.3 (by month for the first year), 3.4 (by quarter for years 2 and 3) and 3.5 (three-year summary).

You want your projections to reflect the realities of your business. They are models of your business (as are the cash flow projections in the next chapter), and should 'look' like your business. To achieve this:

1. Take the gross sales and expense figures from your forecasts for the first year. Spread these across Figure 3.3, month by month.

    A. Start by spreading sales. Most businesses have a steady sales pattern that is peculiar to their business. Hotels and guest houses in the north-east have one pattern; in the south-west, quite another. Some businesses concentrate 75 per cent of their sales in the fourth quarter; others are steady throughout the year. You have to know your business cycle – and it must be reflected in your projections. When do you make the sales? Which are the fat months, and which are the lean ones?

    B. Some expenses are used evenly throughout the year. Legal and accounting, salaries, rent, utilities, etc, don't fluctuate much month to month. Take these evenly distributed expenses and divide by 12 to arrive at monthly figures.

    C. Some expenses are seasonal. You may have to hire extra help for Christmas, or to meet other seasonal demands. Take the amount in the forecast and spread it according to your estimate of when the expense will be incurred.

    D. Some expenses can be precisely timed. Acquiring equipment, incurring new borrowing, or paying off an old loan are examples. Build these into your projections. If you won't begin paying a higher rent until June, don't budget that rent in January. Use your common sense.

    E. Some expenses go up and down with sales. To spread these, you have first to spread your revenues, as you did above. Cost of goods sold, for example, is figured on sales. So are credit and collection costs. Check all your variable expenses.

2. Once you have entered the figures for each month, calculate the Gross Margin, Operating Expense, Other Expense, Total Expense, and Profit (Loss) figures for each month. Cross-total to arrive at the yearly figures which will be used in Figure 3.5: *Three-year summary*.

3. Take the year 2 and year 3 forecasts and spread them by quarters. Allocate revenues and expenses to the quarters they appear in. The evenly incurred expenses and so forth are treated just as they are for the monthly projection, except that instead of dividing annual expense totals by 12 you divide the totals by 4. Enter the numbers on Figure 3.4.

Set up this format on 13-column paper.

	Jan	Feb	Mar	Apr	May	...	Dec
Sales							
Wholesale							
Retail							
Total Sales:							
Cost of materials							
Variable labour							
Cost of goods sold							
Gross Margin							
Operating expenses							
Utilities							
Salaries							
NI							
Advertising							
Office supplies							
Insurance							
Maintenance and cleaning							
Legal and accounting							
Delivery							
Licence fees							
Telephone							
Depreciation							
Rent							
Miscellaneous							
Other expenses							
Total operating expenses:							
Other expenses:							
Interest (mortgage)							
Interest (term loan)							
Interest (overdraft)							
Others							
Total other expenses:							
Total Expenses:							
Net Profit (Loss) Pre-Tax:							

Figure 3.3 *Income (profit and loss) projection by month*

Set up this format on 13-column paper.

| | Year 2 Quarter | | | | | Year 3 Quarter | | | | |
	1	2	3	4	Total	1	2	3	4	Total
Sales										
Wholesale										
Retail										
Total Sales:										
Cost of materials										
Variable labour										
Cost of goods sold										
Gross Margin										
Operating expenses										
Utilities										
Salaries										
NI										
Advertising										
Office supplies										
Insurance										
Maintenance and cleaning										
Legal and accounting										
Delivery										
Licence fees										
Telephone										
Depreciation										
Rent										
Miscellaneous										
Other expenses										
Total operating expenses:										
Other expenses:										
Interest (mortgage)										
Interest (term loan)										
Interest (overdraft)										
Others										
Total other expenses:										
Total Expenses:										
Net Profit (Loss) Pre-Tax:										

Figure 3.4 *Income (profit and loss) projection by quarters for years 2 and 3*

Set up this format on 13-column paper.

	Year 1	Year 2	Year 3
Sales			
Wholesale			
Retail			
Total Sales:			
Cost of materials			
Variable labour			
Cost of goods sold			
Gross Margin			
Operating expenses			
Utilities			
Salaries			
NI			
Advertising			
Office supplies			
Insurance			
Maintenance and cleaning			
Legal and accounting			
Delivery			
Licence fees			
Telephone			
Depreciation			
Rent			
Miscellaneous			
Other expenses			
Total operating expenses:			
Other expenses:			
Interest (mortgage)			
Interest (term loan)			
Interest (overdraft)			
Others			
Total other expenses:			
Total Expenses:			
Net Profit (Loss) Pre-Tax:			

Figure 3.5 *Income (profit and loss) projection: three-year summary*

4. The three-year summary is compiled from these first sets of projections. Take the yearly totals for years 1, 2 and 3, and enter them on Figure 3.5.

Once more, note that these projections lend themselves to modelling on a computerised spreadsheet. Check with your bank manager, accountant or other financial advisers – the chances of a minor arithmetical error blasting your budget's rationale is great, especially when you will be trying out different combinations of sales and expense figures to test your ideas.

◀ CHAPTER 4 ▶

PREPARE CASH FLOW PROJECTIONS

If you were to be limited to one financial statement, the cash flow projection would be the one to pick. For a new or growing business it can make the difference between success and failure. For an ongoing business, it can make the difference between growth and stagnation.

Cash flow is the lifeblood of your business.

Your cash flow projection is your most important cash flow control tool because:

1. It is your cash flow budget.
2. It pinpoints your financing needs.
3. It tells you whether and when to seek equity, loans, operating improvement or advice, or to sell off assets.

'Cash flow' is a highly descriptive term. Cash – liquid assets – flows into your business from a limited number of sources. It flows out through a much larger number of costs. Think of it as the lifeblood of your business. You can literally bleed a business – by taking too much cash out at the wrong time, or allowing many small costs to dribble cash away. You can give a business a transfusion: new capital or increased debt. Your job as the owner or manager is to make sure that you protect the cash flow, because positive cash flow (more coming in than going out) is survival, while negative cash flow (more going out than coming in) will sooner or later kill your business.

The cash flow projection (abbreviated to 'cash flow') is more time sensitive than the income projection. It treats all and only cash items. For example, if you pay your insurance bill in four equal instalments, you will have four disbursements (cheque written, sent, and cashed) on your cash flow, while on the income projection 12 equal expenses will be shown. The income projection has non-cash expenses such as depreciation. The cash flow doesn't touch these – but does show principal repayments on loans, which is not an expense item on the income statement. Keep in mind that the cash flow shows the movement of cash in and out of your business, while the income projection shows expenses and revenues as incurred, whether or not cash changes hands. Figure 4.1 *Cash flow management sketch* provides a picture of cash flow.

The cash flow management sketch shows how cash flows in and out of the business over a stated period. Cash flows in from cash sales, collection of debtors, capital injections, etc, and flows out only through cash payments.

Your cash flow highlights the points in the calendar when the cash actually moves. The advantage of knowing ahead of time when more cash is needed is the ability to plan ahead for those outlays and not be forced into hasty, unexpected borrowing to meet cash needs.

Lack of profits won't kill a business immediately. Although in the long run you have to make a profit to keep going, in the short run non-cash expenditures (depreciation, for example) can make your business show a loss, while the cash flow remains positive. Lack of cash to meet trade and other debts will kill your business quickly, unless new cash is found.

You can foresee the effect of new debt far more clearly in the cash flow than in the profit projection. You may be able to find other ways to finance your business operations or minimise your credit needs, given enough notice. Much of the advantage of studying your cash flow projection stems from timing: more options are available to you, at lower costs, with less panic.

Cash is primarily generated by sales. Perhaps your business is all cash – but if you offer any credit (charge accounts, term payments, trade credit) to your customers, you must have a means of telling when those sales will turn into cash-in-hand. The impact of credit policy is blurred in the profit projection, but made very clear in the cash flow projection.

(See Chaepter 6, Control Debtors and Stock, for more detail on credit and collection management.)

If your business is seasonal, the cash flow projection is vital. Liquidity planning is based on the cash flow – for example, in the garment trade, huge stocks are built up against a short, intense selling period. Timing in cash flow control is everything.

Preparing your cash flow projections

Prepare cash flow projections monthly for at least the next year, or until cash flow turns positive for three consecutive months. Quarterly figures will suffice for years 2 and 3. A three-year summary is sometimes presented in a financing proposal, and serves as a helpful guideline in your business planning.

Cash flow projections lend themselves to computerisation. Graphic displays make spreadsheet programs even more valuable, turning your numbers into more easily understood charts and graphs. You can make changes with much greater speed and accuracy than was possible with a sheaf of sharp hb pencils, 13-column accounting paper and a well-worn eraser.

Use the cash flow management sketch (Figure 4.1) to help make sure you don't omit any cash flow item. Add any that are peculiar to your business. All of your disbursements must be recorded on your cash flow – all cash expenses, loan repayments, owner's withdrawals, capital purchases, everything that sucks away cash. Be thorough. Your cheque book can help to remind you of amounts and timing. So can your cash journal (if you have one).

If you plan to expand your business or acquire or replace equipment, enter those costs and their timing. This gives you another chance to review your needs. You may want to apply the same best case/worst case/most likely case approach to acquisitions. Small business owners have been known to make major purchases without adequate consideration of alternatives. If you have to disburse cash, make sure it goes for a legitimate business purpose.

The level of detail to provide is another matter. You may want to break

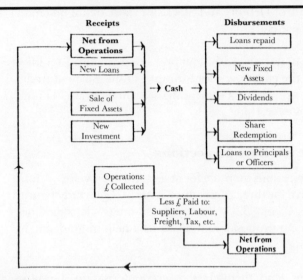

Cash flow sketch

1. **Cash at beginning of period**
   Add revenues, etc:
2. Sales of products (cash)
3. Sales of products (debtors collected)
4. Cash received from assets sold
5. Cash received from equity investment
6. Cash received from loans
7. Cash received from bad debt recovery
8. Miscellaneous cash received
   Total: Cash received

   Subtract: Cash disbursements
9. New stock purchased for cash
10. Salaries/wages
11. VAT
12. Fringe benefits paid
13. New equipment to be purchased for cash
    14. Processing equipment
    15. Office, sales equipment
    16. Transport equipment
17. Insurance premiums
18. Professional fees
    19. Accounting
    20. Legal

21. Utilities
22. Telephone
23. Heat, light, power
24. Advertising
25. Principal and interst on loan
26. Transport
    27. Oil, petrol
    28. Vehicle maintenance
    29. Other running expenses
30. Freight
31. Taxes payable
    32. Income
    33. Corporation
    34. VAT
35. Dividends paid, cash withdrawal by partner, or contribution to profit-sharing plan
36. Provision for unforeseen circumstances (if funded)
37. Provision for replacement of depreciable assets (if funded)

Total cash received Less Total disbursements Equals Cash at end of period

Note. Only cash disbursements are included. These are actual pounds that you pay out, not obligations that you incur now to be paid off at some future date. Those appear on the income projection and balance sheet.

Figure 4.1 *Cash flow management sketch*

the cash flow into a series of cash flows for each profit centre or other business unit. This can be particularly handy if you have more than one major revenue stream, or if you are a manufacturer or contractor and have to prepare numerous bids. (Another plea for computerisation: bid preparation is streamlined by the computer.) The accumulated information gained by several projections can be a very valuable business asset.

Your cash flow projection is a working model of your business, and should reflect the actual patterns of cash use in the business.

As you prepare your cash flow projection, keep these eight points in mind:

1. Prepare the cash flow projection one line at a time, by month for the first year (Figure 4.2), and by quarters for years 2 and 3 (Figure 4.3).
2. Split the sales figures from your income projection into two categories: cash sales and credit sales. You have to plan on the credit sales turning into cash at a later date; how much later (and with what level of bad debt loss) can be predicted on your past experience. Be conservative. If your customers usually pay in 15 days, count on the cash coming in 30 days later. If 30 days is the norm, count on a 45-day return. Cash sales are entered in the month of the sale. Cash receipts, however, will include credit sales from last month, not credit sales from the current month.
3. Cash receipts include cash flowing in from new investment, loans, bad debt recovery, and miscellaneous sources, including the sale of fixed assets. Enter the amounts in the right months.
4. Some of your cash disbursements will be the same each month. (See Finestkind's cash flow projection in Appendix 1.) There is little virtue in entering the same figures in 12 monthly columns for Rent, Salaries, Tax, and similar items that don't change. Lump them together (but provide a display so they can be broken down for closer scrutiny).
5. For all other items, put the disbursement in the month where the actual cash transaction occurs. If you pay legal and accounting fees quarterly, enter them in the month you pay the bill. If you buy supplies twice a year, when do you pay for them? If you plan to buy a piece of equipment, when do you have to pay for it – and where will the cash come from? Some bills get paid in greater or lesser amounts during the course of the year – utilities, advertising, and so on. Put down what you expect to pay in the appropriate months.

6. Once all the figures are entered on Figure 4.2, calculate total cash received, total disbursements, and cash flow. A positive cash flow shows more coming in than going out. A negative cash flow is one where more goes out than comes in.

7. Use the same approach to handle the quarterly cash flow projections for years 2 and 3 in Figure 4.3. Your cash flow projection is a working model of your business, and should reflect the actual patterns of cash use in the business.

8. The three-year summary (Figure 4.3) is derived from Figures 4.2 and 4.3.

Set up this format on 13-column paper.

	Jan	Feb	Mar	...	Dec	Total
Receipts						
Sales receivable						
Wholesale						
Retail						
Other services						
(see notes)						
Total Cash Receipts:						
Cash Disbursements						
Cost of goods						
Variable labour						
Advertising						
Insurance						
Legal and accounting						
Delivery						
Fixed cash disbursements*						
Mortgage (rent)						
Term loan						
Overdraft						
VAT						
Other (see notes)						
Total Cash Disbursements:						
Net Cash Flow:						
Cumulative Cash Flow:						

	Jan	Feb	Mar	...	Dec	Total
Cash in Hand						
Opening balance						
+ Cash received						
– Cash disbursed						
New Balance:						
Total						
Fixed cash disbursements*/year						
Fixed cash disbursements*/Month						
*Fixed cash disbursements						
Utilities						
Salaries						
NI						
Office supplies						
Maintenance and cleaning						
Licence fees						
Telephone						
Rates						
Other						

Figure 4.2   *Cash flow projection by month*

Set up this format on 13-column paper.

	Year 2 Quarter					Year 3 Quarter				
	1	2	3	4	Total	1	2	3	4	Total
Receipts										
Sales receivable										
Wholesale										
Retail										
Other services										
(see notes)										
Total Cash Receipts:										
Cash Disbursements										
Cost of goods										
Variable labour										

	Year 2 Quarter					Year 3 Quarter				
	1	2	3	4	Total	1	2	3	4	Total
Advertising										
Insurance										
Legal and accounting										
Delivery										
Fixed cash disbursements*										
Mortgage (rent)										
Term loan										
Overdraft										
VAT										
Other (see notes)										
Total Cash Disbursements:										
Net Cash Flow:										
Cumulative Cash Flow:										
Cash in Hand										
Opening balance										
+ Cash received										
– Cash disbursed										
New Balance:										
Total										
Fixed cash disbursements*/year										
Fixed cash disbursements*/month										
*Fixed cash disbursements										
Utilities										
Salaries										
NI										
Office supplies										
Maintenance and cleaning										
Licence fees										
Telephone										
Rates										
Other										

Figure 4.3 *Cash flow projection by quarter for years 2 and 3*

Set up this format on 13-column paper.

	Year 1	Year 2	Year 3
Receipts			
Sales receivable			
Wholesale			
Retail			
Other services			
(see notes)			
Total Cash Receipts:			
Cash Disbursements			
Cost of goods			
Variable labour			
Advertising			
Insurance			
Legal and accounting			
Delivery			
Fixed cash disbursements*			
Mortgage (rent)			
Term loan			
Overdraft			
VAT			
Other (see notes)			
Total Cash Disbursements:			
Net Cash Flow:			
Cumulative Cash Flow:			
Cash in Hand			
Opening balance			
+ Cash received			
− Cash disbursed			
New Balance:			
Total			
Fixed cash disbursements*/year			
Fixed cash disbursements*/month			

*Fixed cash disbursements

	Year 1	Year 2	Year 3
Utilities			
Salaries			
NI			
Office supplies			
Maintenance and cleaning			
Licence fees			
Telephone			
Rates			
Other			

Figure 4.4   *Cash flow projection: three-year summary*

◄ CHAPTER 5 ►

USE THE CASH FLOW BUDGET AND VARIANCE ANALYSIS

Your cash flow and profit projections are budgets which help to keep your business heading towards your goals. Of the two, the cash flow budget is the most important. If you meet its forecasts, you will meet the profitability goals implicit in the profit projection, and have cash left over to build the business with.

A budget is a guide that helps you to maintain your business's focus.

You create your budget under optimal conditions. All the information you have, with time to reflect upon it, improved by review and experience, gives you a sound budget. As mentioned earlier, anyone can set up a budget. The trick is to set up a budget worth following, and the step-by-step approach should have given this to you.

When you deviate from your budget, as you will, most likely you will do so under less than ideal conditions – panic, confusion, hustle and bustle, constant interruptions.

Decisions made under stress are seldom as fruitful as those made under calmer conditions. When a major change is forced upon you from outside, take notes keep a notebook to record your reasons, your response, and what happens – whether you made the right decision or not. This will help when you prepare the next version of your budget.

Do this faithfully. It pays off. You will develop:

1. An excellent source of current information;

Since you now know how much cash you need, when you need it, and for how long, you have the beginnings of a powerful financing proposal.

2. An accurate test of the projections you prepared; and

3. A fix on trends, both good and bad, that affect your business.

As you track actual versus projected performance, resist the urge to tinker too often with the budget. A budget is a guide that helps you to maintain your business's focus. On the other hand, a budget shouldn't be a straitjacket. If you have sufficient reason to change your budgets, go ahead.

You may want to cast budgets (cash flow projections) every month, only one quarter at a time (yet another argument for a computerised spreadsheet approach). Each month, forecast and project for the next three months. This compresses your budgeting experience and vaults you up the learning curve. The monthly feedback on your old budgets guarantees better insight into the budgeting process.

By checking actual against budgeted figures each month, you will gain a heightened awareness of short-term trends, both in your business and in the general economy. For instance, personnel turnover will make a small business waver from its projections. As new personnel work into their jobs and become less demanding of more experienced personnel, productivity will rebound and the business will return to its projected course.

Review your achievements and budgets on a monthly basis, but don't change the budget unless your review suggests a major error in your projections. A budget is designed to assist in the normal operations of your business, not in unpredictable variations which are felt only for a week or a month. Keep a log of these extraordinary events, because seen from a longer view, they may form a subtle pattern to help you in the future.

What should you do if all cash outflows are justified and on time, yet planned cash inflow is inadequate? Then you have no choice. You have to generate additional cash somehow. With your cash flow budget at hand, this problem, while severe, is not insurmountable. You can establish a plan for positive cash flow based on facts, not terror.

1. *Examine the cash flow disbursements one by one*, looking for those items which can be rescheduled to ease your cash flow. Perhaps some creditor payments can be renegotiated with your suppliers – they want you to stay in business. It is cheaper for them to help you over a rough spot than to develop a brand new customer. Insurance premiums might be stretched from quarterly to monthly, for example.

2. *Make a list of the disbursements which cannot be changed to other dates.* Salaries and taxes are on this list. Maybe you have to pare back operations, or reduce staff. While these may be last resorts, they should be considered.

3. *List anticipated cash inflows, allowing a margin for safety.* Maybe you can lean on your customers

to pay in 30 instead of 45 days. Maybe you can get a large customer to prepay in exchange for a discount.

4. *Go back to the items you can reschedule.* Do not forget to take full advantage of trade credit, but do not abuse it. Maybe some of these disbursements can be postponed, or eliminated, by tightening up and making do with other assets.

What happens if you still have shortfalls? Congratulate yourself for being realistic. The shortfall indicates a need for some kind of financing. Your cash flow gives you the amount, timing and duration of the financing need.

Since you now know how much cash you need, when you need it, and for how long, you have the beginnings of a powerful financing proposal.

Your well documented cash flow budget is the heart of your financing proposal. It demonstrates that you know what you're doing and that you plan ahead and take all due precautions. Such careful management appeals to bank managers.

Why? The cash flow budgeting process shows that you care enough about the future of your company to establish goals and the controls and routes to reach those goals. The implied discipline is impressive.

Figure 5.1 *Creating monthly budgets*

Variance analysis

Variance analysis is a simple concept. You use your one-year and monthly cash flow and income projections as budgets, test actual against budgeted performance monthly, and flag any variance from the budget. You will want to set some kinds of norm: a 20 per cent variance on any cash inflow or disbursement item would certainly call for your attention. Some managers flag any 5 per cent variance and exercise their judgement as to what to do with each one. Choose your own trigger points, in pounds or percentages.

Choose your own trigger points, in pounds or percentages.

The great advantage is that you will review monthly performance against the budget each month. You can identify opportunities and problems in time to turn them to your advantage.

The four budget variance forms (Figures 5.2–5.5) are easy to use – feel free to copy them. Fill in the projected amounts, fill in the actual performance, and compare them.

| From the Profit and Loss Statement
For the month of _____ | | | |
A Actual for month	B Budget for month	C Variance (B – A)	D % Variance (C/B × 100)
Sales			
Less Cost of Goods			
Gross Profit on Sales			

Operating Expenses:
Variable Expenses
   Sales salaries (commissions)
   Advertising
   Miscellaneous variable			

Total Variable Expenses			

Fixed Expenses
   Utilities
   Salaries
   NI
   Office supplies
   Insurance
   Maintenance and cleaning
   Legal and accounting
   Delivery
   Licences
   Boxes, paper, etc
   Telephone
   Miscellaneous
   Depreciation
   Interest			

Total Fixed Expenses			
Total Operating Expenses			
Net Profit (Gross Profit on Sales less Total Operating Expenses)			
Tax			
Net Profit After Tax			

Figure 5.2 *Budget variance analysis by month*

| | From the Profit and Loss Statement
Year-to-date _____ | | | |
	A Actual for year-to-date	B Budget for year-to-date	C Variance (B – A)	D % Variance (C/B × 100)
Sales				
Less Cost of Goods				
Gross Profit on Sales				
Operating Expenses: **Variable Expenses** Sales salaries (commissions) Advertising Miscellaneous variable				
Total Variable Expenses				
Fixed Expenses Utilities Salaries NI Office supplies Insurance Maintenance and cleaning Legal and accounting Delivery Licences Boxes, paper, etc Telephone Miscellaneous Depreciation Interest				
Total Fixed Expenses				
Total Operating Expenses				
Net Profit (Gross Profit on Sales less Total Operating Expenses)				
Tax				
Net Profit After Tax				

Calculations: A. Add current month actual to last month's year-to-date analysis.
B. Add current month budget to last month's year-to-date analysis.

Figure 5.3   *Budget variance analysis year-to-date*

| | From the Cash Flow For the month of _____ | | | |
	A Actual for month	B Budget for month	C Variance (B – A)	D % Variance (C/B × 100)
Opening Cash Balance				
Add: Cash sales				
Debtors that have turned to cash				
Other cash inflows				
Total Available Cash				
Deduct Estimated Disbursements: Cost of materials Variable labour Advertising Insurance Legal and accounting Delivery Equipment* Loan payments Mortgage payment Rates VAT **Deduct Fixed Cash Disbursements:** Utilities Salaries NI Office supplies Maintenance and cleaning Licences Boxes, paper, etc Telephone Miscellaneous				
Total Disbursements				
Closing Cash Balance				

* Equipment expense represents actual expenditures made for purchase of equipment.

Figure 5.4 *Budget variance analysis by month*

	From the Cash Flow Year-to-date _____			
	A Actual for year-to-date	**B** Budget for year-to-date	**C** Variance (B – A)	**D** % Variance (C/B × 100)
Opening Cash Balance				
Add: Sales revenue				
Other revenue				
Total Available Cash				
Deduct Estimated Disbursements: Cost of materials Variable labour Advertising Insurance Legal and accounting Delivery Equipment* Loan payments Mortgage payment Rates VAT				
Deduct Fixed Cash Disbursements: Utilities Salaries PAYE and NI Office supplies Maintenance and cleaning Licences Boxes, paper, etc Telephone Miscellaneous				
Total Disbursements				
Closing Cash Balance				

Calculations: A. Add current month actual to last month's year-to-date analysis.
B. Add current month budget to last month's year-to-date analysis.
* Equipment expense represents actual expenditure made for purchase of equipment.

Figure 5.5   *Budget variance analysis year-to-date*

◄ CHAPTER 6 ►

CONTROL DEBTORS AND STOCK

The aim is profitability and positive cash flow, not sales increases.

Two of your largest current assets are debtors and stock. In order to manage your cash flow, you want to turn these into cash as soon as possible. However, unless they are managed with cash flow in mind, they can become hidden cash drains.

To manage these assets properly, you must know:

1. The age of your debtors and stock;
2. The turn of your debtors and stock;
3. The concentration of your debtors (how many customers, what value they each represent, what products the balances cover); and
4. The concentration of your stock by product lines.

You must also know what effect your credit and collection policies have on your working capital and cash flow. Small business owners all too often mistake sales for profits. They extend more and more credit, practise lax collection policies, and end up providing interest-free loans to their customers in the name of 'increasing sales'. Many business owners have found that their largest accounts actually cost them money because of slow payment.

No small business owner can afford to provide interest-free loans to his or her biggest customers, but unless you take the time to analyse the payment behaviour of your slow-paying accounts, you may not know what is eating up your cash flow.

This is not to say 'Don't increase credit sales.' The aim is profitability and positive cash flow, not sales increases. If the sales don't translate into bottom-line profits, then you are buying trouble as fast as you are buying sales.

Debtor management

Begin by examining the age of your debtors every week. This helps you to spot the slow-paying accounts early, so you can begin collection efforts as soon as possible.

Separate invoices into current, 30 days old, 60 days, 90 days and over. This is called 'aging the debtors'. You want to set up your aging schedule on the credit terms you offer – current, 10 day, and so on. The main idea is to spot those customers who pay within term (so you can find more of them) and those who do not (so you can re-educate or avoid them in the future).

Then work out your collection period. Divide annual credit sales (from your historical figures or from projections) by 360 to find the average daily credit sale. Next, divide your current outstanding debtors total by the average daily credit sale figure. This gives you your current debtors collection period.

Don't forget to consider seasonality. If sales tend to cluster, your debtors will peak at the time of sales and distort the collection picture. Department stores, for example, have huge debtor balances at the beginning of the year, much smaller balances in the late spring.

A rule of thumb: if your collection period is more than one-third greater than your credit terms (for example, 40 days if your terms are net-30), you have a cash cycle or collection problem that needs your immediate attention.

Follow these five steps in debtors management:
1. *Age your debtors.*
2. *Calculate your collection period.* Use the rule of thumb to check for problems.
3. *Identify and vigorously pursue the slow-paying customers.*
4. *Identify and try to find more fast-paying or term-paying accounts.*

If your collection period is more than one-third greater than your credit terms, you have a cash cycle or collection problem that needs your immediate attention.

5. *Measure the impact of your credit and collection policies on your cash flow by playing 'what-if' with your projections.* Perhaps changing your terms could improve cash flow and profits.

Here is the formula to determine the length of your collection period. These figures come from Finestkind's profit projection in Appendix 1 on page 72.

> Yearly sales:
> | | |
> |---|---|
> | Wholesale | £90,000 |
> | Retail | £126,000 |
> | Total sales: | £216,000 |

The first number to determine is the average daily credit sale. This is reached by dividing total annual credit sales by 360. In Finestkind's case, the retail sales are same-day cash sales. Of the wholesale accounts, let us assume that £43,200, or 20 per cent of total sales, are on credit:

The average daily credit sale is: £43,200/360 = £120.

Once the average daily credit sale is determined, divide it into the current outstanding debtors to find the collection period. Assume that Finestkind's debtor balance figure is £5,000: £5,000/£120 = 41.6 days.

The result is that Finestkind is maintaininig a 41.6-day collection period. This does not look bad – if their terms were net-30. Unhappily, their terms are net-10, so this is well beyond acceptable limits. The higher this collection period climbs, the more Finestkind will find itself getting out of the seafood business and into the banking business. Finestkind's management knows more about fish than financing, and should capitalise on that knowledge.

Credit and collection

The cost of extending credit is a good example of the hidden costs that devour working capital. Most small business owners are not credit experts. They grant credit because other businesses do, and often fail to understand what the impact on profits and cash flow will be. Few small businesses have explicit credit and collection policies, so they lose twice: granting the credit, and then having to collect funds later. If you establish credit and collection policies appropriate to your business, you will increase profits, improve the quality of your current assets, and speed up your cash flow. Check, with your bank manager, accountant, or other qualified professional and get the help and interest you deserve.

Investigate the use of credit cards. These cost little in return for the headaches they can save you. Consider the cost, in direct bad-debt losses as well as in time, effort, and attention that slow-paying accounts cost you. Then add the costs of capital tied up in debtors to the interest you pay to carry those debtors. Is it worth it? Probably not – but you can get a pounds and pence answer from your accountant.

The cost of extending credit is a god example of the hidden costs that devour working capital.

Inventory management

Carrying costs of stock can run as high as 30 per cent of average stock balances, a substantial drain on working capital. Add the costs of insurance, storage, spoilage, pilferage, handling and maintenance to the cost of stock loans. It adds up fast.

It is hard to determine the right amounts of stock to carry. The balance is between stockout and unnecessary expenses, compounded by supplier delivery and reorder times. Some of the factors that your inventory policies should reflect (in addition to the marketing and sales factors, which are dominant) are:

1. *How often do you turn (sell) your stock?* How does that compare with other businesses in your industry?

   You can calculate your stock-turnover ratios by following these formulas:

   Cost of Goods Sold/Average Stock (in £) = Stock Turnover

   Number of Days in Period*/Stock Turnover = Stock Turnover Days

   Cost of Goods Sold/Industry Average Turnover = Industry Average Stock Balance

   *360 days = 1 year, 180 days = 6 months, 30 days = 1 month.
2. *What is your reorder time?* The difference between a 10-day reorder time and a 210-day reorder is enormous, and will affect the level of reserve inventory you carry.
3. *Who are your suppliers?* Where are they located? Delivery times are important.

4. *What trade terms do your suppliers give you?* Taking a 2 per cent discount on 30-day trading terms is equivalent to earning a 72 per cent annual yield. That is considerably more than the interest your bank charges – and has implications for your ordering and inventory policies.

Your job is to run your business, not to become a financing expert.

For some businesses, a 'reserve-for-purchases' policy helps to keep the cost of stock down. Check with your accountant, bank manager or financial adviser.

Remember, your job is to run your business, not to become a financing expert. The correlation between business success and use of outside financial advisers is too well documented to ignore.

◀ CHAPTER 7 ▶

MANAGING POSITIVE CASH FLOW

Positive cash flow – the increase of cash in your business over a period of time – can come from a number of sources. Not all of them are due to good management.

Not all sources of positive cash flow are beneficial or long-term.

You could experience excellent cash flow while going broke:

1. Stop paying your bills. While this may look good from a cash flow viewpoint, it will put you out of business.
2. Forget to pay taxes. More than one business has learned that borrowing from the government is foolish, expensive and illegal.
3. Get a substantial amount of cash from a credulous investor. He or she may not realise that your enterprise is failing.

And so on. Not all sources of positive cash flow are beneficial or long term.

Positive cash flow can come from neutral sources:

1. You have just landed a major contract and the retainer was paid in advance.
2. Your business is seasonal, and this is the time of year when cash rolls in.
3. You accrue funds all year long to make a lump-sum payment into a pension plan and the bill is due next month.

And so on. Positive cash flow usually results from a combination of these neutral sources, with some operating profits tossed in.

The ideal sources of positive cash flow are the ones we all strive for:

1. You really are making a lot of money.
2. Sales are up, costs are down.
3. Prior investments pay off.

The top priority is usually reduction of short-term debt.

Basically, positive cash flow comes from four sources:

1. New investment;
2. New loans;
3. Sale of assets, including sale/leasebacks; and
4. Operating profits.

The first three are limited, because if the fourth does not chip in regularly, you run out of investors, your creditors pull the plug, and you will have no more assets to sell.

Hence the need to carefully ascertain where your positive cash flow is coming from.

Once you've identified the sources, your strategies for using the excess cash can be formulated – but not before. For example, if the sources are a new contract, operating efficiencies due to investment in new equipment, and your ascent up the learning curve, plus a few deferred expenses, you might choose an aggressive strategy. However, if the sources are unpaid bills, unpaid taxes, and sale of your one money-making division, a far different strategy is in order.

Your strategy has to reflect your anticipated cash flows, too. You may find, for instance, that some of the idle cash can be salted away for future growth, while some has to be kept liquid to meet next month's anticipated cash shortfall.

How should you manage your surplus cash?

1. *Establish priorities.* Positive cash flow from operations creates opportunities to make more money.

    Look at the rates of return of available options. Those items with the greatest potential impact on your bottom line are those which either increase revenues (without driving fixed costs out of sight) or decrease expenses. New equipment might further both goals. Reducing loans is always an option. So is increasing advertising and marketing.

The top priority is usually reduction of short-term debt. It is easier to deposit cash against an overdraft than to invest it wisely. Any money not needed for immediate requirements (bringing trade bills payments up to date, paying taxes, meeting the payroll) should be used to pay off short-term debt for two reasons:

    A. You will save substantial interest costs.

    B. Your bank manager will be more amenable to increasing your overdraft if he or she can see periods when your line of credit was only partially extended.

2. *Research investment strategies and opportunities.* There are all too many ways to invest excess cash.

    Some of the questions to ask yourself, once immediate priorities have been satisfied and short-term debt paid out, concern:

    A. *Security.* How safe is my money? Will it be there when I need it?

    B. *Liquidity.* While high-rate, long-term certificates of deposit have their uses, what happens if I need money next month, not two years from now?

    C. *Yield.* Before investing, would the money earn more if reinvested in my company than if it were put in a cash management account? Or would a short-term investment provide the right mix of yield and liquidity for my company at this time?

Keep your aims clear. You want safety and liquidity first, then yield. This doesn't mean letting excess cash sit idle – just that your business should be making its profits on operations, not investments.

3. *Choose the appropriate strategy and stick to it.* Based on your analysis of your business's cash flow and financing needs, you can begin to maximise returns on your excess cash. Be consistent, and be sure that your strategies are in line with your business plan.

◄ SUMMARY ►

Factual, detailed information is needed to run your business.

Controlling cash flow is not mysterious at all. The tools you use are accurate financial information and forecasts based on your experience and your company's historical performance.

If you don't have clear, accurate, timely financial information, you need a new accountant. Information – factual, detailed information – is needed to run your business.

Your cash flow management strategies depend on your business plan. What are your goals? What resources do you have available? What are your financial needs, personnel needs, marketing needs? All of these reflect different systems in your business. Each one influences the others, so in a very real sense it doesn't pay to devote all of your attention to one or a few. All need to be managed.

In other words, your cash flow strategy must be an extension of your business plan. Cash flow control involves more than money flowing in and out of your business. It involves every aspect of your entire business.

APPENDICES

◀ APPENDIX 1 ▶

FINESTKIND SEAFOODS' FINANCIAL STATEMENTS

The Balance Sheet

Balance sheets are designed to show how the assets, liabilities and net worth of a company are distributed at a given point in time. The format is standardised to facilitate analysis and comparison – do not deviate from it.

Balance sheets for all companies, great and small, contain the same categories arranged in the same order. The difference is one of detail. Your balance sheet should be designed with your business information needs in mind. These will differ according to the kind of business you are in, the size of your business, and the amount of information which your bookkeeping and accounting systems make available.

The categories can be defined more precisely. However, the order of the categories is important and you should follow it. They are arranged in order of increasing liquidity (for assets) and decreasing immediacy (for liabilities).

A brief description of each principal category follows:

1. **Tangible Fixed Assets:** land, plant, equipment, leasehold improvements, other items which have an expected useful business life measured in years. Depreciation is applied to those fixed assets which (unlike land) will wear out. The fixed asset value of a depreciable item is shown as the net of cost minus accumulated depreciation.

Balance sheets for all companies contain the same categories arranged in the same order.

The categories are arranged in order of increasing liquidity (for assets) and decreasing immediacy (for liabilities).

```
                        Name of Business
                    Date (day, month, year)
                        Balance Sheet
                                                    £              £
Fixed Assets
Tangible Fixed Assets                                              x
Less: Accumulated Depreciation                                   (x)
Net Tangible Fixed Assets                                         x
Other Fixed Assets                                                x

Current Assets                                      x
Current Liabilities                               (x)
Net Current Assets/(Liabilities)                                  x

Total Assets Less Current Liabilities                            x

Long-term Liabilities                                           (x)

Net Assets                                                       x

Shareholders' Funds: Shares                        x
                     Retained Profits              x
                     Capital Reserves              x              x

Notes to the Balance Sheet
```

Sample Balance Sheet Format

2. **Other Fixed Assets:** intangible assets such as patents, copyrights, exclusive use contracts, loans from directors and employees.
3. **Current Assets:** cash, government securities, marketable securities, loans (other than from directors or employees), debtors, stock, prepaid expenses, any other item which will or could be converted into cash in the normal course of business within one year.
4. **Current Liabilities:** creditors, loans, accrued expenses, wages, salaries, PAYE, VAT, current portion of long-term debt, other obligations coming due within one year.
5. **Long-term Liabilities:** mortgages, trust deeds, intermediate and long-term bank loans, equipment loans (all of these net of the current portion of long-term debt, which appears as a current liability).
6. **Net Assets:** shareholders' funds, retained earnings, other equity, such as capital reserves.

7. **Notes to the balance sheet:** you should provide displays of any extraordinary item (for example, a schedule of creditors). Contingent liabilities such as pending lawsuits should be included in the footnotes. Changes of accounting practices would also be mentioned here.

If you need to provide more detail, do so – but remember to follow the standard format. If you are a limited company you will need to have an audit. Normally the accounts, including the balance sheet, would be assembled by an accountant as well. If you are not a limited company there is no strict legal requirement for an audit in most cases. However, the decision to use a qualified accountant should be made having fully considered the taxation, legal and practical matters involved.

A sample balance sheet for Finestkind follows on the next page.

The balance sheet for Finestkind is modestly detailed. No depreciation has been charged, for example, because the business has just been started. The Shareholders' funds section could have been more complex. The important thing to notice is that it provides a level of detail appropriate for the purposes of the principals, who own all the shares.

> The balance sheet for Finestkind provides a level of detail appropriate for the purposes of the principals, who own all of the shares.

Some financing sources (banks or other investors) may want to see balance sheets projected for each quarter for the first year of operation and annually for the next two. This would quickly show changes in debt, net worth, and the general condition of the business, and could be another helpful control document. You may wish to have a monthly balance sheet (easily done with a microcomputer-powered accounting system), but for many businesses, a year-end balance sheet is all that is required.

Profit Projections

Explanation for Profit Projections Statement
This section will:
  A. Explain how the figures on the projection were calculated.
  B. Detail the assumptions which were made. Numerical references have been made by line – for example, (21) Maintenance and Cleaning.

> The degree of pessimism you should build into a projection is a matter of judgement.

Finestkind Seafoods Limited
1 October 19—

Balance Sheet

	£	£	£
Fixed Assets			
Fixtures and leasehold improvements (d)			13,265
Building (freezer)			4,500
Equipment			3,115
Trucks			6,500
Total Fixed Assets			27,380
Current Assets			
Stock for resale		3,900	
Consumable stores		450	
Debtors		1,700	
Prepaid expenses		320	
Cash		2,150	
		8,520	
Less: Current Liabilities			
Creditors	8,077		
Loans payable in less than 1 year	1,440	(9,517)	
Net Current Liabilities			(997)
Total Assets less Current Liabilities			26,383
Long-term Liabilities			
Deferred creditor (a)		535	
Bank loan (b)		1,360	
Other long-term loans (c)		9,250	(11,145)
Net Assets			£15,238
Shareholders' Funds			£15,238

Notes to Balance Sheet

Accounts payable display:		
Eldredge's Ltd	£3,700	
Lesswing's	4,119	
Paxstone	180	
B&B Refrigeration	78	
	£8,077	

(a) Dave N Hall for electrical work.
(b) Term loan secured by 1974 Landrover, 1983 Ford.
(c) S & S Finance Ltd, Anytown, Middx.
(d) Includes £10,000 in improvements since June. See appraisal in Supporting Document section.

(3) **Sales** include sales of seafood and ancillary products, such as seasonings, sauces, baitbags, bait. In the future, some tourist items may be included.

(4) **Wholesale** and (5) **Retail**. Finestkind plans to service the wholesale trade more extensively than is shown here, although the trend has been built into the calculations. Owing to a major marketing effort (see (18) **Advertising** below), wholesale sales should increase to 60 per cent of gross sales within two years. Retail sales are expected to be more volatile than the wholesale business, levelling off around £20,000 per month owing to space restrictions. Volatility is seasonal, building from late March to a late summer peak. The increases shown in (4) **Wholesale** are based both on the greater number of restaurants open in the summer and the intense marketing efforts, planned for the winter months, to sell directly to the many restaurants which don't yet know Finestkind. Wholesale sales for September of the preceding year were £9,600, so these figures are perhaps more conservative than they need to be.

(4) **Wholesale** in Years 2 and 3 follow the same pattern as Year 1 (seasonality) but start at £10,000/October Year 2 as the result of advertising and marketing efforts, longer experience with the wholesale market, and greater exposure to the market. Year 3 is a bit more seasonal, reflecting a flattening out of the sales curve.

The degree of pessimism you should build into a projection is a matter of judgement. Some is good; too much can be bad, as it will distort a reasonably good game plan and make a realistic deal look too risky.

(6) **Total Sales**. (4) plus (5).

(8) **Cost of Materials**. Finestkind's stock has an average cost of 68 per cent of sales (including a start-up spoilage rate of 5 per cent which has been reduced to under 1 per cent of sales), and has been calculated as 72 per cent of sales to allow for the fluctuation of dockside prices during the winter.

(9) **Variable Labour**. In Years 1 and 2, two part-time summer helpers will be needed: a counter hand at £4/hour for 16 hours/week for 10 weeks, and a fish cutter at £6.75/hour for 20 hours/week for 16 weeks. In Year 3, two full-time counter hands and a full-time cutter will be needed for 10 and 16 weeks, respectively.

(10) **Cost of Goods Sold**. (8) plus (9).

(12) **Gross Margin**. (6) minus (10).

(14) **Operating Expenses**. These are (by and large) the fixed expenses, those which don't vary directly with sales levels. Keeping control of operating expenses is immensely important and easily ovelooked, perhaps because so much emphasis is placed on generating sales. A profitable business needs to control costs and maintain (or increase) sales.

(15) **Utilities**. Prorated by agreement with the utility companies. Goes from £165/month (Year 1) to £220 to £240 in Year 3. It will probably change as new equipment and better insulation are installed.

(16) **Salaries**.
> Year 1: £950/month for Gosling and Swan
> Year 2: £1,200/month for Gosling and Swan
> £850/month for a full-time employee
> Year 3: £1,500/month for Gosling and Swan
> £900/month (£50/month rise) for employee

Salaries are lower than Finestkind would pay for a professional manager in order to preserve scarce capital (they are undercapitalised, and the salaries reflect 'sweat equity'). As the business grows, they hope to take annual bonuses based on profits – after capital needs are met.

(17) **National Insurance**. 12.5 per cent of (16) (approximate figure).

(18) **Advertising**. Local newspaper and radio spots. This is an expense that Finestkind might profitably increase. They reason (correctly) that a consistent, though modest, campaign will be more productive than sporadic, intensive promotions. The advertising budget is 2.5 per cent of (6) **Total Sales**. In Year 1, a large one-off promotional blitz will be made in April to build off-season wholesale business.

(20) **Insurance**. Includes third party liability, employee liability, vehicle and other normal forms of insurance. As the business can afford it, they will add key person disability to the life insurance coverage. Year 2 reflects the increase in employee liability and the property insurances.

(21) **Maintenance and Cleaning**. Mainly supplies – a food market must meet stringent health codes.

(22) **Legal and Accounting**. Retainers to solicitor and accountant, used to smooth out cash flow. Otherwise occasional large bills would distort monthly income projection figures, even though the use of these services is spread evenly over the year.

(23) **Delivery Expenses**. Delivery of merchandise to restaurants and other markets. Year 2: 2 per cent of total sales; Year 3: 1.7 per cent. As the wholesale business increases, route efficiency should also increase, causing delivery expenses to decrease as a percentage of sales.

Keeping control of operating expenses is immensely important and easily overlooked, perhaps because so much emphasis is placed on generating sales.

(24) **Licences**. Payable to professional bodies, local authorities etc.

(25) **Boxes, Paper, etc**. Packaging supplies, which are a semi-fixed expense.

(26) **Telephone**. Needed for sales, pricing, contacting suppliers and markets.

(27) **Depreciation**. Five-year, straight-line on equipment (beginning April, Year 1); straight-line 19 years on building (beginning January, Year 1). These are based on the assumption that 1/5 and 1/19 respectively will be 'used up' in the normal course of doing business. Some businesses try to set this sum aside as a replacement fund.

(28) **Miscellaneous**. Operating expenses too small to be itemised.

(29) **Rent**. Applicable for three months in Year 1; will be replaced by (33) **Mortgage Interest** on the income statement. The principal payments show up on the cash flow projections as part of mortgage payments. (The £876 per month includes both principal and interest. Principal payments on loans do not appear as income statement items.)

(30) **Total Operating Expenses**. Total of (15) to (29) inclusive.

(32) **Other Expenses**. Non-operating costs are broken down to give them special prominence.

(33) **Interest (Mortgage)**. £75,000 mortgage for 15 years at 11.5 per cent. This is a normal term and interest rate for commercial buildings at this time. More than 15 years is rare.

(34) **Interest (Term Loan)** £30,000 loan for seven years at 12.25 per cent. A rule of thumb: the longer the term, the higher the risk to the bank – so the higher the interest rate to you.

(35) **Interest Overdraft**. Estimated use of overdraft: average of £7,500 outstanding for six months a year at 13.5 per cent. Overdrafts are not intended to replace permanent capital or long-term credit needs.

(36) **Total Other Expenses**. Total of (33), (34), (35).

(37) **Total Expenses**. Total of (30) and (36).

(39) **Net Profit (Loss) Pre-Tax**. (12) **Gross Margin** minus (37) **Total Expenses**. On this statement (and the other projections) a tax liability should be imputed. We left that liability off as it will vary depending on the tax rates in force and with the legal structure of your business. Make sure to check with your accountant to arrive at a true net profit (loss) figure. As one bank manager puts it, 'There is no such thing as a pre-tax profit.'

Finestkind does not expect to make much money for the first few years. This is no surprise for a business so thinly capitalised. Even if there were no debt at all, net profit would have been only £8,000 for the year, or less than 4 per cent of sales.

This is a projection based on conservative figures. In their more optimistic moments, Gosling and Swan hope to hold fixed costs to £4,500 per month, not the £5,200 projected, and increase sales 12.5 per cent. Their budgeted net profit would be around £18,000, not the projected loss of £4,540. If their gross margin were to continue at 30 per cent of sales, not the 28 per cent projected, their net profit would be over £18,000, their 'best-case' assumption.

One item which should be mentioned again is rent. The cost of space appears on the cash flow as mortgage (£876/month). Another is loan amortisation, which also appears on the cash flow as term loan (£534/

month). These include interest and debt repayment, which are not expenses since they are for capital improvements that will be written off as 'depreciation expense' over the course of several years. It is important not to double-deduct expenses. Such a practice is not only illegal but also obscures the information about your business.

Information is the most valuable result of financial statements. Accurate, timely information helps you to run your business.

Information is the most valuable result of financial statements.

Cash Flow Projections

Explanation for cash flow projections

The receipts shown on these cash flow projections include both sales and other cash sources to emphasise their impact on Finestkind. The cash flow projections show how business operations affect cash flow, so some people prefer to isolate 'Other Sources' of cash receipts in the cash reconciliation section (lines (40)–(43) in the Year 1 Cash Flow Projection). References are to line numbers on the accounting sheet unless otherwise noted.

(3) **Sales Receivable**. Sales are cash for retail, cash or 10-day net for wholesale accounts. If Finestkind provided longer terms, their cash flow could be significantly altered. As it is, the cash flow assumes a conservative 10-day lag on all wholesale sales. Since wholesale sales in September were £6,000, £2,000 (10/30 of September wholesale sales) turns to cash in October.

The same rationale applies to the rest of the year: one-third of wholesale receipts aren't collected until the following month.

The collection lag is not continued beyond the first quarter of Year 2. Experience will correct the cash flow, and new figures should be calculated for Year 2 on a monthly basis for Year 2 business planning.

(4) **Wholesale**. Note the total of £28,700 + 60,100 (Total Sales Receivable and Total Wholesale) = £88,800, which is £1,200 less than the projected sales of £90,000 shown on the income statement. To reconcile the difference between these figures, note that £2,000 in cash receipts come from September of the preceding year, while £3,200 of

Profit Projection by Month, Year 1

	A	B	C	D	E	F
1		October	November	December	January	February
2		£	£	£	£	£
3	Sales					
4	Wholesale	4,000	4,000	5,200	5,600	6,000
5	Retail	9,730	9,500	9,500	9,000	8,400
6	**Total Sales:**	**13,730**	**13,500**	**14,700**	**14,600**	**14,400**
7						
8	Cost of Materials	9,885	9,720	10,584	10,512	10,368
9	Variable Labour					
10	Cost of Goods Sold	9,885	9,720	10,584	10,512	10,368
11						
12	**Gross Margin**	**3,845**	**3,780**	**4,116**	**4,098**	**4,032**
13						
14	Operating Expenses					
15	Utilities	160	165	180	200	200
16	Salaries	1,900	1,900	1,900	1,900	1,900
17	National Insurance	237	238	237	238	237
18	Advertising	450	450	450	450	450
19	Office Supplies	25	25	25	25	25
20	Insurance	70	70	70	110	110
21	Maintenance and Cleaning	25	25	25	25	25
22	Legal and Accounting	125	125	125	125	125
23	Delivery Expenses	150	150	150	150	150
24	Licences	9	9	9	9	9
25	Boxes, Paper, etc	15	15	15	15	20
26	Telephone	85	85	85	85	85
27	Depreciation	0	0	0	455	460
28	Miscellaneous					
29	Rent	550	550	550	0	0
30	Total Operating Expenses:	3,841	3,847	3,861	3,827	3,836
31						
32	Other Expenses					
33	Interest (Mortgage)	0	0	0	695	695
34	Interest (Term Loan)	0	0	0	0	0
35	Interest (Overdraft)	0	85	85	0	0
36	Total Other Expenses:	0	85	85	695	695
37	**Total Expenses:**	**3,841**	**3,932**	**3,946**	**4,522**	**4,531**
38						
39	**Net Profit (Loss) Pre-Tax:**	**4**	**(152)**	**170**	**(434)**	**(499)**
40						
41						
42						
43						

This spreadsheet was prepared using the Excel spreadsheet program from Microsoft.®

G	H	I	J	K	L	M	N
March	April	May	June	July	August	September	Total
£	£	£	£	£	£	£	£
7,000	7,000	8,400	10,600	11,300	11,300	9,600	90,000
8,750	10,300	11,540	12,165	12,165	12,475	12,475	126,000
15,750	17,300	19,940	22,765	23,465	23,775	22,075	216,000
11,340	12,456	14,357	16,391	16,895	17,118	15,894	155,520
			604	796	796	604	2,800
11,340	12,456	14,357	16,995	17,691	17,914	16,498	158,320
4,410	4,844	5,583	5,770	5,774	5,861	5,577	57,690
180	170	165	185	185	185	185	2,160
1,900	1,900	1,900	1,900	1,900	1,900	1,900	22,800
238	237	238	237	238	237	238	2,850
450	4,605	450	450	450	450	450	9,555
25	25	25	25	25	25	25	300
110	110	110	110	110	110	110	1,200
25	25	25	25	25	25	25	300
125	125	125	125	125	125	125	1,500
150	150	150	150	150	150	150	1,800
10	10	10	10	10	10	10	115
35	40	45	50	50	50	50	400
85	85	85	85	85	85	85	1,020
460	1,050	1,055	1,055	1,055	1,055	1,055	7,700
							0
0	0	0	0	0	0	1,650	3,300
3,833	8,572	4,423	4,447	4,448	4,447	4,448	53,830
							0
							0
696	695	695	696	695	695	696	6,258
0	272	272	272	272	272	272	1,632
0	0	0	165	165	0	0	500
696	967	967	1,133	1,132	967	968	8,390
4,529	9,539	5,390	5,580	5,580	5,414	5,416	62,220
(119)	(4,695)	193	190	194	447	161	(4,540)
	Cumulative						
	Loss:						
	(5,725)						
	Low Point						

Profit Projection by Quarter, Year 2

	A	B	C	D	E	F
1		1st Quarter	2nd Quarter	3rd Quarter	4th Quarter	Total
2		£	£	£	£	£
3	Sales					
4	Wholesale	38,900	54,800	76,500	94,800	265,000
5	Retail	41,000	37,400	48,600	53,000	180,000
6	**Total Sales:**	**79,900**	**92,200**	**125,100**	**147,800**	**445,000**
7						
8	Cost of Materials	57,528	66,384	90,072	106,416	320,400
9	Variable Labour	0	0	604	2,196	2,800
10	Cost of Goods Sold	57,528	66,384	90,676	108,612	323,200
11						
12	**Gross Margin**	**22,372**	**25,816**	**34,424**	**39,188**	**121,800**
13						
14	Operating Expenses					
15	Utilities	660	660	660	660	2,640
16	Salaries	9,750	9,750	9,750	9,750	39,000
17	National Insurance	1,218	1,218	1,219	1,220	4,875
18	Advertising	2,000	2,305	3,125	3,695	11,125
19	Office Supplies	90	90	90	90	360
20	Insurance	950	950	950	950	3,800
21	Maintenance and Cleaning	90	90	90	90	360
22	Legal and Accounting	500	500	500	500	2,000
23	Delivery Expenses	1,598	1,844	2,502	2,956	8,900
24	Licences	25	30	30	30	115
25	Boxes, Paper, etc	150	175	225	250	800
26	Telephone	450	450	450	450	1,800
27	Depreciation	3,125	3,125	3,125	3,125	12,500
28	Miscellaneous	150	150	150	150	600
29	Rent					
30	Total Operating Expenses:	20,756	21,337	22,866	23,916	88,875
31						
32	Other Expenses					0
33	Interest (Mortgage)	2,070	2,070	2,070	2,070	8,280
34	Interest (Term Loan)	798	798	797	796	3,189
35	Interest (Overdraft)			140	360	500
36	Total Other Expenses:	2,868	2,868	3,007	3,226	11,969
37	**Total Expenses:**	**23,624**	**24,205**	**25,873**	**27,142**	**100,844**
38						
39	**Net Profit (Loss) Pre-Tax:**	**(1,252)**	**1,611**	**8,551**	**12,046**	**20,956**

This spreadsheet was prepared using the Excel spreadsheet program from Microsoft.®

Profit Projection by Quarter, Year 3

	A	B	C	D	E	F
		1st Quarter	2nd Quarter	3rd Quarter	4th Quarter	Total
1		1st Quarter	2nd Quarter	3rd Quarter	4th Quarter	Total
2		£	£	£	£	£
3	Sales					
4	Wholesale	58,750	55,000	97,500	113,750	325,000
5	Retail	47,400	43,600	56,000	63,000	210,000
6	**Total Sales:**	**106,150**	**98,600**	**153,500**	**176,750**	**535,000**
7						
8	Cost of Materials	76,428	70,992	110,520	127,260	385,200
9	Variable Labour	0	0	1,622	5,898	7,520
10	Cost of Goods Sold	76,428	70,992	112,142	133,158	392,720
11						
12	**Gross Margin**	**29,722**	**27,608**	**41,358**	**43,592**	**142,280**
13						
14	Operating Expenses					
15	Utilities	720	720	720	720	2,880
16	Salaries	11,700	11,700	11,700	11,700	46,800
17	National Insurance	1,462	1,462	1,463	1,463	5,850
18	Advertising	2,655	2,465	3,835	4,420	13,375
19	Office Supplies	120	120	120	120	480
20	Insurance	1,025	1,025	1,025	1,025	4,100
21	Maintenance and Cleaning	105	105	105	105	420
22	Legal and Accounting	625	625	625	625	2,500
23	Delivery Expenses	1,805	1,675	2,610	3,010	9,100
24	Licences	25	30	30	30	115
25	Boxes, Paper, etc	200	200	350	450	1,200
26	Telephone	600	600	600	600	2,400
27	Depreciation	3,125	3,125	3,125	3,125	12,500
28	Miscellaneous	180	180	180	180	720
29	Rent					
30	Total Operating Expenses:	24,347	24,032	26,488	27,573	102,440
31						
32	Other Expenses					
33	Interest (Mortgage)	2,013	2,013	2,013	2,013	8,052
34	Interest (Term Loan)	725	725	725	725	2,900
35	Interest (Overdraft)			140	360	500
36	Total Other Expenses:	2,738	2,738	2,878	3,098	11,452
37	**Total Expenses:**	**27,085**	**26,770**	**29,366**	**30,671**	**113,892**
38						
39	**Net Profit (Loss) Pre-Tax:**	**2,637**	**838**	**11,992**	**12,921**	**28,388**

This spreadsheet was prepared using the Excel spreadsheet program from Microsoft.®

Profit Projection: Three-Year Summary

	A	B	C	D
		Year 1	Year 2	Year 3
1		Year 1	Year 2	Year 3
2		£	£	£
3	Sales			
4	Wholesale	90,000	265,000	325,000
5	Retail	126,000	180,000	210,000
6	**Total Sales:**	**216,000**	**445,000**	**535,000**
7				
8	V* Cost of Materials	155,520	320,400	385,200
9	V Variable Labour	2,800	2,800	7,520
10	Cost of Goods Sold	158,320	323,200	392,720
11				
12	**Gross Margin**	**57,680**	**121,800**	**142,280**
13				
14	Operating Expenses			
15	F Utilities	2,160	2,640	2,880
16	F Salaries	22,800	39,000	46,800
17	V/F National Insurance	2,850	4,875	5,850
18	F Advertising	9,555	11,125	13,375
19	F Office Supplies	300	360	480
20	F Insurance	1,200	3,800	4,100
21	F Maintenance and Cleaning	300	360	420
22	F Legal and Accounting	1,500	2,000	2,500
23	V/F Delivery Expenses	1,800	8,900	9,100
24	F Licences	115	115	115
25	V/F Boxes, Paper, etc	400	800	1,200
26	F Telephone	1,020	1,800	2,400
27	F Depreciation	7,700	12,500	12,500
28	F Miscellaneous	480	600	720
29	F Rent	1,650	0	0
30	Total Operating Expenses:	53,830	88,875	102,440
31				
32	Other Expenses			
33	Interest (Mortgage)	6,258	8,280	8,052
34	Interest (Term Loan)	1,632	3,189	2,900
35	Interest (Overdraft)	500	500	500
36	Total Other Expenses:	8,390	11,969	11,452
37	**Total Expenses:**	**62,220**	**100,844**	**113,892**
38				
39	**Net Profit (Loss) Pre-Tax:**	**(4,540)**	**20,956**	**28,388**
40				
41	*V = Variable Cost, F = Fixed Cost			

This spreadsheet was prepared using the Excel spreadsheet program from Microsoft.®

cash receipts are postponed for September of Year 1. Sales figures are based on the Profit Projections on pages 72 to 76.

(5) **Retail**. See Profit Projections on pages 72 to 76.

(6) **Other Sources**

October.	Stock loan using overdraft
November.	Closing costs, using overdraft
January.	Purchase building; £30,000 from Gosling and Swan as new equity investment, along with a £75,000 mortgage
April.	Equipment and building improvements, from term loan
June.	Stock loan, overdraft

(7) **Total**. Cash Receipts are the sum of (3) + (4) + (5) + (6). Note that the total is distorted by loans and new investment.

(8) **Cash Disbursements**. These are the disbursements which will be made in cash (including cheques) during the normal course of business plus any major anticipated cash outlays.

(9) **Cost of Goods**. From Profit Projection on page 72, line 10.

(10) **Variable Labour**. From Profit Projection on page 72, line 9.

(11) **Advertising**. Budgeted at £400 per month for the first year, plus an extra £600 in September for a tourist-oriented advertising campaign and an extra £4,155 in April to an agency for the major wholesale marketing programme, including implementation and execution.

(12) **Insurance**. Payable quarterly.

(13) **Legal and Accounting**. Payable quarterly.

(14) **Delivery Expenses**. Varies with volume of wholesale sales.

(15) **Fixed Cash Disbursements**. These are relatively independent of sales, so they are allocated evenly throughout the year. See display on lines (26) to (37) for details. If salaries fluctuate widely, break them out

as a separate item with the other disbursements. For example, if you meet your payroll every other week, two months of the year will have three paydays rather than two, which can make those months look alarmingly costly.

(16) **Mortgage** (rent). Rent to December at £550 per month, mortgage payments (principal and interest) at £876 thereafter.

(17) **Term Loan**. £535 per month for seven years, which includes principal and interest.

(18) **Overdraft**. Includes principal repayment and interest.

(19) **Other**

January.   Purchasing building
March.   Equipment purchase and building improvements to be paid in full.

(20) **Total Cash Disbursements**. Sum of lines (9) to (19).

(22) **Net Cash Flow**. (7) minus (20).

(24) **Cumulative Cash Flow**. (22) + last month's (24). This sums up the net cash flow on a monthly basis, adding the present month's net cash flow to last month's cumulative cash flow. This is useful on a periodic basis (monthly or quarterly). Over a longer time, it's of academic interest only.

Some experts advise projecting a cash flow until the cumulative cash flow is consistently positive.

(39)–(43) **Cash Balance Reconciliation**. (40) + (41) – (42) = (43). This display (for Year 1 only) may be used as a quick check on how well the budget is doing. For Years 2 and 3, it is not accurate enough to be useful.

Notes and Explanations for
Finestkind Seafoods Limited
Cash Flow Projection by Month, Year 1

Further explanation of these cash flow items appears on the notes supporting the profit projections, on pages 65 to 71.

(3) **Sales Receivable**. Our terms are cash retail, net 10 days for wholesale accounts. Assumes one-third of wholesale will turn to cash in the following month.

(4) **Wholesale**. See profit projections for derivation of these figures.

(5) **Retail**. See profit projections for derivation.

(6) **Other Sources**. October, November overdraft, £7,500; January £75,000 mortgage and £30,000 new equity from Swan and Gosling; April term loan for improvements and equipment, £30,000; June inventory build-up, £15,000 from credit line.

(9) **Cost of Goods**. 72 per cent of current month sales (line (6) of profit projections).

(10) **Variable Labour**. Part-time help from May to September to handle extra weekend tourist trade and extra seafood preparation.

(11) **Advertising**. £1,000 initial burst, £400 per month thereafter. Add £4,155 to April for whole marketing programme.

(16) **Mortgage**. £550 per month rent to December, mortgage payments January on. Terms: £75,000, 15 year, 11.5 per cent.

(17) **Term Loan**. £534 per month payments scheduled for term loan. Terms: £30,000, seven year, 12.25 per cent.

Notes and Explanations for
Finestkind Seafoods Limited
Cash Flow Projection by Quarters
for Years 2 and 3

(4) **Receipts** represent payments from debtors for September, Year 1. Since this is a quarterly summary, no further allowance will be made for the delay in receipts.

(7) **Other Sources**. £12,000 for one month on overdraft third quarter, £15,000 for nine weeks on overdraft fourth quarter to meet stock needs.

Cash Flow Projection by Month, Year 1

	A	B	C	D	E	F
		October	November	December	January	February
1		£	£	£	£	£
2	Cash Receipts					
3	Sales Receivable	2,000	1,350	1,350	1,750	1,850
4	Wholesale	2,650	2,650	3,450	3,750	4,000
5	Retail	9,730	9,500	9,500	9,000	8,400
6	Other Sources (see notes)	7,500	7,500		105,000	
7	**Total Cash Receipts:**	**21,880**	**21,000**	**14,300**	**119,500**	**14,250**
8	Cash Disbursements					
9	Cost of Goods	9,885	9,720	10,584	10,512	10,368
10	Variable Labour					
11	Advertising	1,000	400	400	400	400
12	Insurance		300			300
13	Legal and Accounting			375		
14	Delivery Expenses	75	75	75	100	75
15	Fixed Cash Disbursements*	2,535	2,535	2,535	2,535	2,535
16	Mortgage (rent)	550	550	550	876	876
17	Term Loan					
18	Overdraft		85	15,085		
19	Other (see notes)				105,000	
20	**Total Cash Disbursements:**	**14,045**	**13,665**	**29,604**	**119,423**	**14,554**
21						
22	**Net Cash Flow:**	**7,835**	**7,335**	**(15,304)**	**77**	**(304)**
23						
24	**Cumulative Cash Flow:**	**7,835**	**15,170**	**(134)**	**(57)**	**(361)**
25						
26	**Fixed Cash Disbursements**	**(FCD)**				
27	Utilities	2,160				
28	Salaries	22,800				
29	PAYE and NI	2,850				
30	Office Supplies	300				
31	Maintenance and Cleaning	300				
32	Licences	115				
33	Boxes, Paper, etc	400				
34	Telephone	1,020				
35	Miscellaneous	480				
36	Total: FCD/yr	30,425				
37	FCD/mo	2,535				
38						
39	**Cash in Hand**					
40	Opening Balance	2,150	9,905	17,240	1,936	2,013
41	+ Cash Receipts	21,800	21,000	14,300	119,500	14,250
42	– Cash Disbursements	14,045	13,665	29,604	119,423	14,554
43	Total = New Balance	9,905	17,240	1,936	2,013	1,709

This spreadsheet was prepared using the Excel spreadsheet program from Microsoft.®

G	H	I	J	K	L	M	N
March	April	May	June	July	August	September	Total
£	£	£	£	£	£	£	£
2,000	2,300	2,300	2,800	3,500	3,750	3,750	28,700
4,700	4,700	5,600	7,100	7,550	7,550	6,400	60,100
8,750	10,300	11,540	12,165	12,165	12,475	12,475	126,000
	30,000		15,000				165,000
15,450	47,300	19,440	37,065	23,215	23,775	22,625	379,800
11,340	12,456	14,357	16,391	16,895	17,118	15,894	155,520
			604	796	796	604	2,800
400	4,555	400	400	400	400	400	9,555
		300			300		1,200
375			375			375	1,500
100	150	200	200	250	250	250	1,800
2,535	2,535	2,535	2,535	2,535	2,535	2,540	30,425
876	876	876	876	876	876	876	9,534
	534	534	534	534	534	534	3,204
			165	165	15,000		30,500
30,000							135,000
45,626	21,106	19,202	22,080	22,451	37,809	21,473	381,038
(30,176)	26,194	238	14,985	764	(14,034)	1,152	(1,238)
(30,537)	(4,343)	(4,105)	10,880	11,644	(2,390)	(1,238)	
1,709	(28,467)	(2,273)	(2,035)	12,950	13,714	(320)	
15,450	47,300	19,440	37,065	23,215	23,775	22,625	379,800
45,626	21,106	19,202	22,080	22,451	37,809	21,473	381,038
(28,467)	(2,273)	(2,035)	12,950	13,714	(320)	832	

Cash Flow Projection by Quarter, Year 2

	A	B	C	D	E	F
		1st Quarter	2nd Quarter	3rd Quarter	4th Quarter	Total
1		£	£	£	£	£
2	Cash Receipts					
3	Receipts from debtors	3,200				3,200
4	Wholesale	38,900	54,800	76,500	94,800	265,000
5	Retail	41,000	37,400	48,600	53,000	180,000
6	Other Sources			12,000	15,000	27,000
7	**Total Cash Receipts:**	**83,100**	**92,200**	**137,100**	**162,800**	**475,200**
8	Cash Disbursements					
9	Cost of Goods	57,528	66,384	90,072	106,416	320,400
10	Variable Labour			604	2,196	2,800
11	Advertising	2,000	2,305	3,125	3,695	11,125
12	Insurance	950	950	950	950	3,800
13	Legal and Accounting	500	500	500	500	2,000
14	Delivery Expenses	1,600	1,844	2,500	2,956	8,900
15	* Fixed Cash Disbursements	12,630	12,640	12,640	12,640	50,550
16	Mortgage (rent)	2,628	2,628	2,628	2,628	10,512
17	Term Loan	1,602	1,602	1,602	1,602	6,408
18	Overdraft			12,140	15,360	27,500
19	Other (see notes)					
20	**Total Cash Disbursements:**	**79,438**	**88,853**	**126,761**	**148,943**	**443,995**
21						
22	**Net Cash Flow:**	**3,662**	**3,347**	**10,339**	**13,857**	**31,205**
23						
24	**Cumulative Cash Flow:**	**2,424**	**5,771**	**16,110**	**29,967**	**54,272**
25						
26	*** Fixed Cash Disbursements**					
27	**(FCD)**	Year 2				
28	Utilities	2,640				
29	Salaries	39,000				
30	National Insurance	4,875				
31	Office Supplies	360				
32	Maintenance and Cleaning	360				
33	Licences	115				
34	Boxes, Paper, etc	800				
35	Telephone	1,800				
36	Miscellaneous	600				
37	Total: FCD/yr	50,550				
38	FCD/qtr	12,638				

This spreadsheet was prepared using the Excel spreadsheet program from Microsoft.®

Cash Flow Projection by Quarter, Year 3

	A	B	C	D	E	F
		1st Quarter	2nd Quarter	3rd Quarter	4th Quarter	Total
1						
2	Cash Receipts	£	£	£	£	£
3	Receipts from debtors					325,000
4	Wholesale	58,750	55,000	97,500	113,750	535,000
5	Retail	47,400	43,600	56,000	63,000	162,600
6	Other Sources			12,000	15,000	27,000
7	**Total Cash Receipts:**	**106,150**	**98,600**	**165,500**	**191,750**	**562,000**
8	Cash Disbursements					
9	Cost of Goods	76,428	70,992	110,520	127,260	385,200
10	Variable Labour			1,622	5,898	7,520
11	Advertising	2,655	2,465	3,835	4,420	13,375
12	Insurance	1,025	1,025	1,025	1,025	4,100
13	Legal and Accounting	625	625	625	625	2,500
14	Delivery Expenses	1,805	1,675	2,610	3,010	9,100
15	* Fixed Cash Disbursements	15,215	15,215	15,215	15,220	60,865
16	Mortgage (rent)	2,628	2,628	2,628	2,628	10,512
17	Term Loan	1,602	1,602	1,602	1,602	6,408
18	Overdraft			12,140	15,360	27,500
19	Other (see notes)					
20	**Total Cash Disbursements:**	**101,983**	**96,227**	**151,822**	**177,048**	**527,080**
21						
22	**Net Cash Flow:**	**4,167**	**2,373**	**13,678**	**14,702**	**34,920**
23						
24	**Cumulative Cash Flow:**	**4,167**	**8,334**	**10,707**	**24,385**	**47,593**
25						
26	*** Fixed Cash Disbursements**					
27	**(FCD)**	Year 3				
28	Utilities	2,880				
29	Salaries	46,800				
30	National Insurance	5,850				
31	Office Supplies	480				
32	Maintenance and Cleaning	420				
33	Licences	115				
34	Boxes, Paper, etc	1,200				
35	Telephone	2,400				
36	Miscellaneous	720				
37	Total: FCD/yr	60,865				
38	FCD/qtr	15,216				

This spreadsheet was prepared using the Excel spreadsheet program from Microsoft.®

(16) **Fixed Cash Disbursements**. Could have included mortgage and term loan payments, but to preserve parity with detail of Year 1, loan payments are displayed separately.

(24) **Cumulative Cash Flow**. Subtract £1,238 from net cash flow, first quarter Year 2, to reflect the total cumulative cash flow of Year 1: (£1,238).

(26) **Fixed Cash Disbursements**. From Profit Projections.

You should notice that only the most important cash flow items are annotated. Such annotation helps you remember your thinking at some later time – and helps to avoid repeating errors. It also makes your projections much more believable, since the numbers will be seen to have more foundation than guesswork.

Application of funds statement

This is a handy addition to your cash flow analysis. Your bank manager may be interested in a Source and Applications statement, which is a slightly more formal version – ask your accountant – but this is handy when you are looking at ways of financing major acquisitions.

Use of Funds	Total Amount Required £	From Equity £	From Loans £	From Other £
Acquire building	105,000	30,000	75,000	
Improve building	24,000		20,000	4,000
Equipment	10,000		10,000	

◀ APPENDIX 2 ▶

BIBLIOGRAPHY AND RESOURCES

Further reading from Kogan Page

Kogan Page publishes an extensive list of books for business managers and business owners; those particularly helpful to the reader of this book are likely to be:

The Business Plan Workbook, Colin and Paul Barrow, 1988
Buying for Business: How to Get the Best Deal from Your Suppliers, Tony Attwood, 1988
Debt Collection Made Easy, Peter Buckland, 1987
Financial Management for the Small Business, Colin Barrow, 2nd edition, 1988
How to Cut Your Business Costs, Peter D Brunt, 1988
How to Deal With Your Bank Manager, Geoffrey Sales, 1988
Profits from Improved Productivity, Fiona Halse and John Humphrey, 1988
Raising Finance: The Guardian Guide for the Small Business, Clive Woodcock, 1989

Sources of help and advice

The Small Firms Service
The Small Firms Service, which is provided by the Department of Employment, offers an information and counselling service. It operates through a nataionwide network, with more than a dozen small firms centres backed up by nearly 100 area counselling offices throughout

Great Britain. Counselling can be provided either at a local area office or at your premises and the first three sessions are free. If further sessions are required a modest charge may be made. Contact your local branch by calling the operator on 100 and asking for Freefone Enterprise.

Details of the services provided for their respective communities (including those of the Rural Development Commission) can be found at:

Wales: The Welsh Development Agency (Small Business Unit), Treforest Industrial Estate, Pontypridd, Mid Glamorgan CF37 5UT; 044 385 2666.

Scotland: The Scottish Development Agency, Small Business Division, Rosebery House, Haymarket Terrace, Edinburgh EH12 5EZ; 031-337 9595.

Northern Ireland: Local Enterprise Development Unit, Ledu House, Upper Galwally, Belfast BT8 4TB; 0232 491031.

Other organisations
Alliance of Small Firms and Self-Employed People, 33 The Green, Calne, Wilts SN11 8DJ; 0249 817003.

The Association of British Factors, 147 Fleet Street, London EC4A 2BU; 01-353 1213.

The Chartered Association of Certified Accountants, 29 Lincoln's Inn Fields, London WC2A 3EE; 01-242 6855.

The Association of Invoice Factors, 109-113 Royal Avenue, Belfast BT1 1FF; 0232 24522.

The British Exporters Association, 16 Dartmouth Street, London SW1H 9BL; 01-222 5419.

The Equipment Leasing Association, 18 Upper Grosvenor Street, London W1X 9PB; 01-491 2783.

Export Credits Guarantee Department (ECGD), Headquarters at:

Aldermanbury House, London EC2P 2EL; 01-606 6699.

Institute of Chartered Accountants in England and Wales, PO Box 433, Chartered Accountants Hall, Moorgate Place, London EC2P 2BJ; 01-628 7060.

The Institute of Chartered Accountants of Scotland, 27 Queen Street, Edinburgh EH2 2LA; 031-225 5673.

The Chartered Institute of Management Accountants, 63 Portland Place, London W1N 6AB; 01-637 2311.

The Institute of Directors, 116 Pall Mall, London SW1Y 5ED; 01-839 1233. They represent the interests of both large company directors and the owner/directors of small ones. They run schemes from time to time, putting those with funds in touch with those who need them.

Local enterprise agencies. About 300 local enterprise agencies have been set up specifically to help people starting or already running a small business. These agencies frequently have a small full-time staff seconded from industry or the financial sector. They can offer advice on bookkeeping methods, preparing business plans, raising finance and perhaps even local business courses. Alternatively, you can contact the Industrial Development Officer at your town hall, who will either advise personally or suggest someone else who can.

Training

Training courses for business managers and owners are run by many local education authorities.

Training Agency (previously known as the Manpower Services Commission), Moorfoot, Sheffield S1 4PQ; 0742 753275 supports a wide range of courses designed specifically to help people who are thinking of setting up a new business. Many of their courses include a substantial element of financial training, bookkeeping, costing and planning, and raising money. The courses are run at colleges and business schools throughout the country and over the whole year.

Cranfield School of Management, Cranfield, Bedfordshire MK43 0AL; 0234 751122 runs courses for owner-managers of established businesses.

Profit Projection by Month, Year 1

	A	B	C	D	E	F
		October	November	December	January	February
1						
2		£	£	£	£	£
3	Sales					
4	Wholesale					
5	Retail					
6	**Total Sales:**					
7						
8	Cost of Materials					
9	Variable Labour					
10	Cost of Goods Sold					
11						
12	**Gross Margin**					
13						
14	Operating Expenses					
15	Utilities					
16	Salaries					
17	National Insurance					
18	Advertising					
19	Office Supplies					
20	Insurance					
21	Maintenance and Cleaning					
22	Legal and Accounting					
23	Delivery Expenses					
24	Licences					
25	Boxes, Paper, etc					
26	Telephone					
27	Depreciation					
28	Miscellaneous					
29	Rent					
30	Total Operating Expenses:					
31						
32	Other Expenses					
33	Interest (Mortgage)					
34	Interest (Term Loan)					
35	Interest (Overdraft)					
36	Total Other Expenses:					
37	**Total Expenses:**					
38						
39	**Net Profit (Loss) Pre-Tax:**					
40						
41						
42						
43						

G	H	I	J	K	L	M	N
March	April	May	June	July	August	September	Total
£	£	£	£	£	£	£	£

Profit Projection by Quarter, Year 2

	A	B	C	D	E	F
		1st Quarter	2nd Quarter	3rd Quarter	4th Quarter	Total
1		1st Quarter	2nd Quarter	3rd Quarter	4th Quarter	Total
2		£	£	£	£	£
3	Sales					
4	Wholesale					
5	Retail					
6	**Total Sales:**					
7						
8	Cost of Materials					
9	Variable Labour					
10	Cost of Goods Sold					
11						
12	**Gross Margin**					
13						
14	Operating Expenses					
15	Utilities					
16	Salaries					
17	National Insurance					
18	Advertising					
19	Office Supplies					
20	Insurance					
21	Maintenance and Cleaning					
22	Legal and Accounting					
23	Delivery Expenses					
24	Licences					
25	Boxes, Paper, etc					
26	Telephone					
27	Depreciation					
28	Miscellaneous					
29	Rent					
30	Total Operating Expenses:					
31						
32	Other Expenses					
33	Interest (Mortgage)					
34	Interest (Term Loan)					
35	Interest (Overdraft)					
36	Total Other Expenses:					
37	**Total Expenses:**					
38						
39	**Net Profit (Loss) Pre-Tax:**					

Profit Projection by Quarter, Year 3

	A	B	C	D	E	F
1		1st Quarter	2nd Quarter	3rd Quarter	4th Quarter	Total
2		£	£	£	£	£
3	Sales					
4	Wholesale					
5	Retail					
6	**Total Sales:**					
7						
8	Cost of Materials					
9	Variable Labour					
10	Cost of Goods Sold					
11						
12	**Gross Margin**					
13						
14	Operating Expenses					
15	Utilities					
16	Salaries					
17	National Insurance					
18	Advertising					
19	Office Supplies					
20	Insurance					
21	Maintenance and Cleaning					
22	Legal and Accounting					
23	Delivery Expenses					
24	Licences					
25	Boxes, Paper, etc					
26	Telephone					
27	Depreciation					
28	Miscellaneous					
29	Rent					
30	Total Operating Expenses:					
31						
32	Other Expenses					
33	Interest (Mortgage)					
34	Interest (Term Loan)					
35	Interest (Overdraft)					
36	Total Other Expenses:					
37	**Total Expenses:**					
38						
39	**Net Profit (Loss) Pre-Tax:**					

Cash Flow Projection by Month, Year 1

	A	B	C	D	E	F
		October	November	December	January	February
1						
2	Cash Receipts	£	£	£	£	£
3	Sales Receivable					
4	Wholesale					
5	Retail					
6	Other Sources (see notes)					
7	**Total Cash Receipts:**					
8	Cash Disbursements					
9	Cost of Goods					
10	Variable Labour					
11	Advertising					
12	Insurance					
13	Legal and Accounting					
14	Delivery Expenses					
15	Fixed Cash Disbursements*					
16	Mortgage (rent)					
17	Term Loan					
18	Overdraft					
19	Other (see notes)					
20	**Total Cash Disbursements:**					
21						
22	**Net Cash Flow:**					
23						
24	**Cumulative Cash Flow:**					
25						
26	**Fixed Cash Disbursements**					
27	Utilities					
28	Salaries					
29	PAYE and NI					
30	Office Supplies					
31	Maintenance and Cleaning					
32	Licences					
33	Boxes, Paper, etc					
34	Telephone					
35	Miscellaneous					
36	Total: FCD/yr					
37	FCD/mo					
38						
39	**Cash in Hand**					
40	Opening Balance					
41	+ Cash Receipts					
42	– Cash Disbursements					
43	Total = New Balance					

G	H	I	J	K	L	M	N
March	April	May	June	July	August	September	Total
£	£	£	£	£	£	£	£

Cash Flow Projection by Quarter, Year 2

	A	B	C	D	E	F
		1st Quarter	2nd Quarter	3rd Quarter	4th Quarter	Total
1						
2	Cash Receipts	£	£	£	£	£
3	Receipts from debtors					
4	Wholesale					
5	Retail					
6	Other Sources					
7	**Total Cash Receipts:**					
8	Cash Disbursements					
9	Cost of Goods					
10	Variable Labour					
11	Advertising					
12	Insurance					
13	Legal and Accounting					
14	Delivery Expenses					
15	* Fixed Cash Disbursements					
16	Mortgage (rent)					
17	Term Loan					
18	Overdraft					
19	Other (see notes)					
20	**Total Cash Disbursements:**					
21						
22	**Net Cash Flow:**					
23						
24	**Cumulative Cash Flow:**					
25						
26	*** Fixed Cash Disbursements**					
27	**(FCD)**					
28	Utilities					
29	Salaries					
30	National Insurance					
31	Office Supplies					
32	Maintenance and Cleaning					
33	Licences					
34	Boxes, Paper, etc					
35	Telephone					
36	Miscellaneous					
37	Total: FCD/yr					
38	FCD/qtr					

Cash Flow Projection by Quarter, Year 3

	A	B	C	D	E	F
1		1st Quarter	2nd Quarter	3rd Quarter	4th Quarter	Total
2	Cash Receipts	£	£	£	£	£
3	Receipts from debtors					
4	Wholesale					
5	Retail					
6	Other Sources					
7	**Total Cash Receipts:**					
8	Cash Disbursements					
9	Cost of Goods					
10	Variable Labour					
11	Advertising					
12	Insurance					
13	Legal and Accounting					
14	Delivery Expenses					
15	* Fixed Cash Disbursements					
16	Mortgage (rent)					
17	Term Loan					
18	Overdraft					
19	Other (see notes)					
20	**Total Cash Disbursements:**					
21						
22	**Net Cash Flow:**					
23						
24	**Cumulative Cash Flow:**					
25						
26	*** Fixed Cash Disbursements**					
27	**(FCD)**					
28	Utilities					
29	Salaries					
30	National Insurance					
31	Office Supplies					
32	Maintenance and Cleaning					
33	Licences					
34	Boxes, Paper, etc					
35	Telephone					
36	Miscellaneous					
37	Total: FCD/yr					
38	FCD/qtr					